mustsees
Grand Canyon & Arizona

Canyon Naitonal Park/NPS photo by Kim Besom

MICHELIN

mustsees **Grand Canyon & Arizona**

Editorial Director	Cynthia Clayton Ochterbeck
Editorial Manager	Gwen Cannon
Contributing Writers	Gwen Cannon, Dayton Fandray, Joyce Holly, Eric Lucas, Carey Sweet
Production Manager	Natasha G. George
Cartography	Peter Wrenn
Photo Researcher	Nicole D. Jordan
Layout	Nicole D. Jordan
Additional Layout	Natasha G. George
Cover & Interior Design	Chris Bell, cbdesign
Cover Design & Layout	Natasha G. George
Contact Us	Michelin Travel and Lifestyle North America One Parkway South Greenville, SC 29615, USA travel.lifestyle@us.michelin.com www.michelintravel.com
	Michelin Travel Partner Hannay House 39 Clarendon Road Watford, Herts WD17 1JA, UK www.ViaMichelin.com travelpubsales@uk.michelin.com
Special Sales	For information regarding bulk sales, customized editions and premium sales, please contact us at: travel.lifestyle@us.michelin.com www.michelintravel.com

Michelin Travel Partner
Société par actions simplifiées au capital de 11 629 590 EUR
27 cours de l'Ile Seguin - 92100 Boulogne Billancourt (France)
R.C.S. Nanterre 433 677 721

© 2013 Michelin Travel Partner
ISBN 978-2-067185-03-6
Printed: December 2012
Printed and bound in Italy

Note to the reader:
While every effort is made to ensure that all information printed in this guide is correct
and up-to-date, Michelin Travel Partner accepts no liability for any direct, indirect or
consequential losses howsoever caused so far as such can be excluded by law. Admission
prices listed for sights in this guide are for a single adult, unless otherwise specified.

Welcome to Arizona

Saguaro cactus
Saguaro National Park

©Eye Ubiquitous/Photoshot

p 79

©Kim Morris/Lowell Observatory

p 76

p 119

©Randy Larson

Must Do

Must Eat

Must Stay

Must Know

TABLE OF CONTENTS

★★★ ATTRACTIONS

Unmissable historic, cultural and natural sights

Grand Canyon National Park   p 36

NPS Photo by Michael Quinn

The Heard Museum   p 91

©Craig Smith

Hoover Dam   p 71

©4nadia/iStockphoto.com

Arizona-Sonora Desert Museum, Coati p 115

©Arizona-Sonora Desert Museum

Musical Instrument Museum p 92

Courtesy of MIM

Desert Caballeros Western Museum p 69

©Gwen Cannon/Michelin

★★★ ATTRACTIONS

Unmissable historic, cultural and natural sights

For more than 75 years people have used Michelin stars to take the guesswork out of travel. Our star-rating system helps you make the best decision on where to go, what to do, and what to see.

★★★	Unmissable
★★	Worth a trip
★	Worth a detour
No star	Recommended

MUST KNOW

ACTIVITIES

Unmissable activities, entertainment, restaurants and hotels

Arizona's desert landscapes and remarkable wildlife lend a sense of drama to human activities here. We recommend every activity in this guide, but the Michelin Man logo highlights our top picks.

Outings

Admire Native art
p 69, 75, 91
Behold birds *p 16, 133*
Drive cattle *p 98*
Ferry over a lake *p 68*
Dither at a dam *p 65, 71*
Mosey on a mule *p 46*
Relive history *p 69,
83, 133*
See a shootout *p 82, 129*
Spa the day away *p 110*
Stargaze *p 18, 121, 155*
Take a train *p 42*
Watch a rodeo *p 16-18*

Hotels

Arizona Inn *p 150*
L'Auberge de Sedona
p 144
The Boulders *p 148*
Canyon Ranch *p 150*
Casa de San Pedro *p 151*
Copper Queen Hotel
p 152
Hermosa Inn *p 148*
La Posada *p 146*
El Tovar *p 38*

Nightlife

Arcadia Tavern *p 100*
Blue Hound Kitchen
p 100
Club Congress *p 125*

Four Peaks Brewing
Company *p 100*
Handlebar J *p 100*
Harold's Cave Creek
Corral *p 100*
Heat Hotel bar *p 153*

Ranches

Apache Spirit *p 155*
Caballeros *p 154*
Flying E *p 154*
Saguaro Lake *p 155*
Sunglow *p 155*
Tanque Verde *p 154*
White Stallion *p 155*

Relax

Browse for books *p 124*
Have Mexican food
p 138, 140, 143
Soak in a hot tub *p 147*
Sip afternoon tea *p 150*
Zone out at the zoo
p 62, 95

Restaurants

Binkley's *p 137*
Café Elote *p 136*
Cafe Poca Cosa *p 142*
Café Roka *p 142*
Criollo Latin Kitchen
p 135
Los Dos Molinos *p 141*
Farm Kitchen *p 141*

Local Bistro *p 141*
Prado *p 139*

Shopping

Cowboy boots *p 123*
Leather *p 82, 122*
Native crafts *p 90*
Recyclables *p 123*
Vintage clothing *p 123*
Western art *p 18, 83*

Side Trips

Bryce Canyon NP *p 51*
Cedar Breaks NM *p 53*
Glen Canyon NRA *p 65*
Grand Staircase-
Escalante NM *p 53*
Kodachrome Basin
SP *p 52*
Las Vegas *p 71*
Mesa Verde NP *p 64*
Rainbow Bridge
NM *p 65*
Zion NP *p 49*

Sports

Golfing *p 96*
Hiking *p 97*
Horseback riding *p 98*
Kayaking *p 98*

STAR ATTRACTIONS

IDEAS AND TOURS

Throughout this thematic guide you will find inspiration for many different ways to experience Arizona and the Grand Canyon. The following is a selection of places and activities from the guide to help start you off. The sights in bold are found in the index.

PEAKS AND VALLEYS

Thanks to John Ford and the Westerns he filmed in Monument Valley, Arizona's rugged landscape has come to symbolize the American West in the mind's eye of people around the world. So what better way to discover the West than to explore this awe-inspiring landscape up close and personal? **Monument Valley★★★** sits partially on Navajo Nation land and a trip to this iconic terrain of towering buttes and rock monoliths can also include side trips to **Canyon de Chelly★★**. The latter is a 26mi-long canyon (and National Monument) famous for its well-preserved cliff dwellings and artifacts left by Ancestral Puebloans who lived there and disappeared sometime around 1350 AD. Not far away sits the **Hubbell Trading Post★**, a National Historic Site and the oldest continuously operating trading post on the Navajo reservation. Farther west, the **Grand Canyon★★★** cuts a jagged gash through the earth's crust—one of those rare attractions that actually lives up to its advance billing. The easiest access to **Grand Canyon National Park★★★**, but not the most scenic, is the **South Rim★★★**. Here, visitors can simply stand and gawk, or descend into the canyon on foot or mule-back. Rafting trips on the roiling Colorado River add real adventure to a visit. The more isolated **North Rim★★** can be reached easily from **Las Vegas★★★** or **Flagstaff★**. A visit to the North Rim is also a good jumping-off point for trips to **Zion National Park★★★** and **Bryce Canyon National Park★★★** in nearby Utah. South of the Grand Canyon, the **San Francisco Peaks** tower over **Flagstaff★**, home to **Northern**

Zion National Park

©Caitlin Cec/National Park Service

10

Arizona University. At 12,622ft in elevation, **Humphreys Peak** is the tallest of these peaks, and Arizona's highest point. South of Flagstaff, **Sedona★★** and **Oak Creek Canyon★★** host world-famous red rocks that number among the most-photographed rock formations in the world. The towering red cliffs and the supernatural vortices rumored to converge here have made Sedona a mecca for New Age pilgrims and artists alike.

Although the northern part of the state is arguably the most dramatic in terms of topography, Southern Arizona tantalizes visitors with the evocative rock formations that adorn the peaks of the **Chiricahua Mountains**. Equally inspiring are the sweeping views of Mexico and the San Pedro Valley that are visible from the **Huachuca Mountains** south of Sierra Vista. In Western Arizona, the **Colorado River** emerges from the Grand Canyon and pours into **Lake Mead**, the vast reservoir created by **Hoover Dam★★★**. While the **Lake Mead National Recreation Area★** and the river below Hoover Dam are probably best known for the boating and water sports they facilitate, the river knifes through some spectacular desert country as it runs from the dam on down to the Mexican border.

THE PAST IS PRESENT

Achieving statehood in 1912, Arizona was the last of the 48 contiguous states to enter the Union. So, in one sense, it is a very new and very modern place. But Arizona's history in fact stretches back across the millennia, and thanks largely to its dry climate

Trail riding, Saguaro Lake Guest Ranch

©Saguaro Lake Guest Ranch

and the fact that it was settled so recently, much of that history has been preserved. Native American culture is the starting point for any serious history buff who comes to the Grand Canyon State. It can be seen at sites like **Tuzigoot★** and **Montezuma Castle★** and **Casa Grande Ruins★** national monuments, where Native peoples lived; many of their dwellings and artifacts survive to this day. For a broader view, one that takes in the entire sweep of the Native American presence in Arizona, the best place to start is **The Heard Museum★★★** in Phoenix, a grand repository of Native America art, artifacts, and exhibits that focus on the role indigenous peoples have played in the history of the Southwest. Equally interesting, but a bit more remote, the **Amerind Foundation Museum★** in Cochise County, just east of **Benson**, offers a collection of art and artifacts that puts the Native American experience into both a cultural and historical perspective.

11

The flip side of Indians, of course, is cowboys—and the European explorers and settlers who preceded them. A visit to **Tombstone**★★ brings you face to face with Wyatt Earp, the Clantons, and some of the most potent legends of the American West. "Dude" ranches (see HOTELS), which saw their heyday in Arizona in the 1930s and 40s, afford today's visitors plenty of opportunity to find their inner cowboy (or girl) atop a steed mozying along the Salt River (as at **Saguaro Lake Ranch** near Mesa), on trails in the "backyards" of **Wickenburg**★, home to **Flying E Ranch** and **Rancho de los Caballeros** or at Tucson's famed **Tanque Verde Ranch**.

The San Pedro Valley, which spreads out west of Tombstone, is believed to be the place where a band of conquistadors led by Francisco Vazquez de Coronado first entered present-day Arizona. Searching for seven cities of gold, they brought the land under the control of the Spanish crown. Spanish Colonial influence can be felt throughout Southern Arizona, especially in the ruins of the mission at **Tumacácori**★, now a National Historical Park, and at the "white dove of the desert," **Mission San Xavier del Bac**★★, just south of **Tucson**★★. Southeast of Tucson, the **Bisbee Mining and Historical Museum** preserves Arizona's era as one of the world's great mining centers. Moving into the recent past, Tucson's **Pima Air and Space Museum**★★ celebrates Arizona's role as a hub for aviation, especially during World War II and the Cold War era. Arizona is also home to a long stretch of

what is arguably the most famous highway in the world. **Route 66** crosses the northern part of the state, and even though it has been supplanted largely by Interstate 40, towns like **Kingman**★, **Flagstaff**★, **Williams** and Winslow all pay tribute in their own way to the Mother Road, the great highway that symbolizes the westward drift of the American Dream.

ARTISTIC ARIZONA

The natural beauty of the terrain in Arizona has inspired generations of artists. This muse has long been reflected in the jewelry, baskets and blankets created by the Native peoples. As European settlers moved in to work the land, artists followed as a matter of course. Arizona has influenced painters, sculptors and photographers alike to create memorable artwork. This art can be seen in any number of galleries and museums throughout the state. In **Phoenix**★★, the **Phoenix Art Museum**★★ is a must-see destination for any lover of the arts. While the museum features artwork by both regional and international artists, local artists are well represented in the galleries of **Scottsdale** and the Roosevelt Avenue arts district in downtown Phoenix. **Tucson**★★, too, has a major art museum, the **Tucson Museum of Art & Historic Block**★★. The **Center for Creative Photography**★★ on Tucson's **University of Arizona**★ campus features a world-renowned collection of photography that includes the archives of iconic photographer Ansel Adams. Many artists call Tucson home, and their work can be seen in a growing number of galleries along **4th**

Avenue near the university, as well as downtown in the city's warehouse district. To the north, the red rocks of **Sedona★★** have exerted an irresistible tug on artists for years; the town's galleries draw collectors from every corner of the world. **Bisbee★★**, too, has a lively arts scene; growing numbers of collectors are drawn to the galleries that thrive in this rough-hewn community in the **Mule Mountains** of Cochise County.

WHERE THE WILD THINGS GROW

The **giant saguaro** is the iconic symbol of Arizona. Found only in the **Sonoran Desert**, this towering cactus is a tough survivor that can live through the scorching heat of Arizona's summers, yet endure the freezing temperatures of the desert nights in winter. It is at once menacing, yet on close examination surprisingly delicate, even beautiful. As such, it is typical of both the flora and fauna that thrive in Arizona. From the roadrunner to the prickly pear to the **Gila monster**, the plants and animals in Arizona seem a bit other-worldly, like something that came out of a cartoon or some of the early science-fiction movies, and therefore, especially attractive to anyone in tune with the natural world. The best place to observe them is in the wild, in their natural habitats. Fortunately, there is no shortage of natural habitat. In the northern part of the state, the **Coconino National Forest**, with its grasslands and ample stands of ponderosa pine, is home to red-tailed hawks, porcupines, elk, badgers and coyote. The plants and animals most closely

associated with Arizona, such as cactus, rattlesnakes, javelinas, Gambel's quail, and desert tortoises, can be found at lower elevations, in the central and southern parts of the state. Any of the metropolitan parks around Phoenix like **South Mountain Park Preserve★** and **Camelback Mountain** provide ample chances for encountering native wildlife. In Tucson, the two districts of **Saguaro National Park★★** and **Tucson Mountain Park** afford similar opportunities. Arizona is also a favorite destination for bird watchers and the best viewing is in the south, particularly the **San Pedro Valley** and the **Huachuca and Chiricahua mountains**, which are often referred to as "sky islands" because the high elevations attract birds native to a wide variety of habitats. If meeting the beasties in the wild is a daunting proposition, the **Desert Botanical Garden★★** in Phoenix, the **Arizona-Sonora Desert Museum★★★** in Tucson, and the **Boyce Thompson Arboretum★** in Superior are all magnificent destinations where local wildlife can be comfortably viewed in near-natural habitats.

METRO ARIZONA

There's a lot more to Arizona than rocks and Gila monsters. The state is young, yes, but it is one of the fastest growing in the Union. As the state has grown in population, so has it grown in sophistication. The **Phoenix★★** metropolitan area is dynamic and sophisticated. **Tucson★★**, although a bit more relaxed in outlook, is not far behind. Both cities have symphony orchestras, and the **Arizona Theatre Company** and

13

Night scene, downtown Phoenix

©Greater Phoenix CVB

the **Arizona Opera** shuttle back and forth between them. Given the climate, it comes as no surprise that Phoenix and Tucson both boast world-class golf courses, with the **Troon North Golf Club** in Scottsdale topping many a golfer's list of must-play courses. Where you have golf courses, you are likely to find resorts, and both Phoenix and Tucson have resorts and spas to spare, like the Phoenix area's well-known **The Boulders**, and **Royal Palms Resort and Spa**, and Tucson's **Canyon Ranch** and the historic **Arizona Inn. Sedona★★**, too, is an exquisite setting for a resort experience and it delivers with the delightful **Enchantment Resort**, which nestles unobtrusively at the foot of the area's red rock cliffs. Phoenix fields professional teams in all four major sports— baseball, football, basketball and hockey—and in the spring, the city fairly bursts with spring training action with **Cactus League teams** drawing throngs to stadia in every corner of the Valley.

Fine dining and nightlife are part of the scene in both Phoenix and Tucson. The nationally acclaimed **Vincent on Camelback** in Phoenix and Janos Wilder's **Downtown Kitchen + Cocktails** in Tucson are just two of the thousands of fine restaurants that delight locals and visitors alike. You don't have to stay in the metropolitan areas to enjoy top-notch dining. Restaurants like Bisbee's exquisite **Cafe Roka** can be found in small towns throughout the state.

NORTH OF THE BORDER

When the US acquired Arizona (and New Mexico) in the mid-19C, the Mexican population did not rise en masse and move to the Mexican side of the hastily redrawn border. Many remained, living as they had for years. As American settlers arrived from the East, European and Mexican traditions blended, creating a hybrid culture that is still evolving a decade into the new millennium. Mexican food is probably the most visible manifestation of Mexican-

American culture in Arizona, and one never has to go far to find a good burrito, enchilada, tostada or that culinary darling of the moment, a **Sonoran hot dog**. Mexican restaurants, like **Los Dos Molinos** in Phoenix, Tucson's **Cafe Poca Cosa** and **Bisbee Breakfast Club** in Bisbee abound throughout the state, but locals generally agree that South Tucson is the destination of choice for authentic Sonoran cuisine (think Tucson's **El Minuto** and **El Guero Canelo**). The Phoenix area and northern parts of the state were sparsely settled at the time of annexation, so the Mexican influence on Arizona's culture is best savored in Tucson and Southern Arizona. **Tucson★★** celebrates its Mexican roots in a number of popular annual events (*see Calendar of Events*), the most flamboyant of which is the **All Souls Procession** the weekend following Halloween. With 35,000 costumed participants, music, and floats that push the limits of the imagination, the procession is a spectacle that reframes the Mexican **La Dia de Los Muertos** holiday in a distinctly modern, American context. Held every February, **La Fiesta de Los Vaqueros** is a weeklong rodeo that brings together American and Mexican cowboy traditions. The **Tucson International Mariachi Conference**, in April, celebrates this proud musical tradition through a weekend-long series of workshops and public concerts.

Quick Trips
Stuck for ideas? Try these:

IDEAS AND TOURS

CALENDAR OF EVENTS

Listed below is a selection of Arizona's most popular annual events; some dates may vary from year to year. For detailed information on these and other festivals, contact local tourism offices (numbers listed under individual entries) or access www.arizonaguide.com.

January

Tostitos Fiesta Bowl Football Classic
Glendale, 480-350-9011
www.fiestabowl.org
This post-season college football bowl game brings in the crowds at the University of Phoenix Stadium.

Wings Over Willcox
Willcox, 800-200-2272
www.wingsoverwillcox.com
The popular birding and nature festival focuses on the migrating sandhill cranes that winter in and around Willcox.

February

Accenture Match Play Golf Championship
Marana, 520-207-0595, www.worldgolfchampionships.com
Arizona Renaissance Festival
Gold Canyon, 520-463-2600
www.royalfaires.com
Fanciful costumes and period music bring to life a re-creation of an early English village within a medieval amusement park. Jousting tournaments add fun.

La Fiesta de los Vaqueros
Tucson, 800-964-5662
www.tucsonrodeo.com
Tucson's celebration features one of the nation's top professional rodeos and a parade of horse riders in colorful costumes of the early Southwest.

Tubac Festival of the Arts
Tubac, 520-398-2704
www.tubacaz.com
This event showcases the works of many visiting artists, artisans and musicians.

Tucson Gem & Mineral Show
Tucson, 520-322-5773
www.tgms.org
Internationally famous, the show draws thousands to the city to buy and sell gems, minerals, fossils and jewelry from retailers and private collectors.

February: La Fiesta de los Vaqueros, Tucson

©Louise Serpa

16

April: La Frontera International Mariachi Conference

Tucson International Mariachi Conference

March

Cactus League Spring Training
Greater Phoenix,
www.cactusleague.com

Cowgirl Up!
Wickenburg, 928-684-2272
www.cowgirlupart.com
Art from the women of the West Invitational Exhibition & Sale is spotlighted at this event.

Ostrich Festival
Chandler, 480-963-4571
www.ostrichfestival.com
Ostrich-pulled cart races, ostrich rides, a petting zoo and animal shows headline this 3-day fest.

**Tres Rios Nature &
Earth Festival**
Goodyear, 623-932-2260
www.tresriosnaturefestival.com
The rich nature of the Gila River area is celebrated at this outdoor gathering, open to all ages.

Tucson Festival of Books
Tucson, 520-891-9681
Held on the UA campus, the 2-day event is a nod to books, reading and literacy. Food and activities are geared to appeal to families. Workshops and talks by many current authors are included.

April

**Fiesta Days Rodeo
& Parade**
Cave Creek, 480-488-4043
www.cavecreekrodeo.com

**La Frontera International
Mariachi Conference**
Tucson, 520-838-3908
www.tucsonmariachi.org
Created to pass mariachi traditions to the next generation, the event features workshops for interested students who then give concerts for the public.

**Verde Valley Nature &
Birding Festival**
Cottonwood, 928-282-2202
www.birdyverde.org

**Jesus the Christ Easter
Pageant**
Mesa, 480-654-1077
www.easterpageant.org

May

Historic Home & Building Tour
Jerome, 928-634-2900
www.jeromechamber.com
The annual Historic Home and Building Tour is held mid-May to encourage the public to tour some of Jerome's historic houses and other structures for a look at life in times past in this old mining center.

17

Phippen Museum Western Art Show and Sale

Prescott, 928-778-1385
www.phippenartmuseum.org

This much-anticipated show attracts lovers of **Western art** to the exhibits and sales arranged by the Phippen every year.

Tucson Folk Festival

Tucson, 800-638-8350
www.tkma.org

The Tucson Kitchens Music Association sponsors lively entertainment from national and local artists who demonstrate traditional music and dance.

Zuni Festival of Arts and Culture

Flagstaff, 928-774-5213
www.musnaz.org

June

Cowpunchers Reunion Rodeo

Williams, 928-853-6495
www.williamschamber.com

This popular annual event teams up with the Northern Arizona Barbeque Festival to offer spectators exciting food as well as thrills in the arena.

Grand Canyon Star Party

South Rim, Grand Canyon
520-792-6414, tucsonastronomy.org/gcsp.html

Telescopes are on hand for the public to view the spectacular night sky over the canyon.

Prescott Frontier Days and World's Oldest Rodeo

Prescott, 928-445-3103
www.worldsoldestrodeo.com

Saguaro Harvest Festival

Vail, 520-647-7275
www.colossalcave.com

Treaty Days Celebration

Window Rock, 928-871-7055
www.navajonationfair.com

July

Bisbee 4th of July Parade

Bisbee, 520-432-6004

At the oldest July 4th parade in the state, activities include coaster races down winding streets as well as competitions among miners.

Hopi Festival of Arts & Culture

Flagstaff, 928-774-5213
www.musnaz.org

White Mountains Roundup of Cowboy Poetry, Music & Art

Pinetop/Lakeside, 928-367-0240
www.whitemountainsroundup.com

August

Southwest Wings Birding & Nature Festival

Sierra Vista, 520-678-8237
www.swwings.org

Hummingbirds are some of the smallest and most fascinating birds to visit this region of southeastern Arizona. Birders also come to spot raptors, quail, flycatchers and songbirds that are usually prevalent during the period this annual event is held.

May: Tucson Folk Festival

©MJStringerPhoto.com, 2009

September

Oktoberfest on Mt. Lemmon
Tucson, 520-576-1400
Among the pines and aspens high above the city of Tucson, German beer and food, music, and dancing can be found at Mt. Lemmon Ski Valley.

Rendezvous of Gunfighters
Tombstone, 888-457-3929
www.tombstonechamber.com

SalsaFest
Safford, 928-428-2511
www.salsatrail.com

Standin'on the Corner Festival
Winslow,
www.standinonthecorner.com

Vertielee Floyd Memorial Old Time Fiddlers Contest Arizona State Championship
Payson, 928-474-4515
www.paysonrimcountry.com

October

Anza Days
Tubac, 520-398-2252
This living-history event, held in Presidio State Park, is complete with re-enactments, mariachi music, musket demonstrations, and fun activities for kids.

Helldorado Days
Tombstone, 888-457-3929
www.helldoradodays.com
Tombstone's oldest festival hails the town's world-famous shoot'em-up days of the past.

Patagonia Fall Festival
Patagonia, 888-794-0060
An art show and festival pay tribute to autumn in this pretty valley south of Tucson.

Tucson Meet Yourself
Tucson, 520-792-4806
A downtown salute to Southern Arizona's folk and ethnic heritage, this event offers traditional arts, ethnic food and entertainment.

November

Page Lake Powell Hot Air Balloon Regatta
Page, 928-660-3405,
www.pagelakepowelltourism.com

All Souls Procession
Tucson, 800-638-8350
This singular annual parade presents a host of community members, many costumed in amazing attire, as part of the Day of the Dead celebration. The finale is usually a high-wire spectacle of lights, fire and acrobatics.

Holiday Nights at Tohono Chul Park
Tucson, 520-742-6455
The Sonoran Desert botanical garden sparkles with thousands of lights placed throughout Tohono Chul Park for the holiday season. It's a memorable sight.

December

Downtown Tucson Parade of Lights
Tucson, 520-882-8585
This holiday parade features unusual entries as well as seasonal music and festivities. Sponsored by the Downtown Tucson Partnership.

Glendale Glitters
Glendale, 623-930-2299
www.glendaleaz.com

Great Pinecone Drop
Flagstaff, 800-842-7293
www.flagstaffarizona.org
A metal pinecone is dropped from Hotel Weatherford's balcony in Flagstaff's version of New York's Times Square ball drop.

Pueblo Grande Museum Indian Market
Phoenix, 602-495-0901
wwwpgindianmarket.com

PRACTICAL INFORMATION

WHEN TO GO

Save for the higher elevations in the northern part, the Grand Canyon State is pretty much a year-round destination. Most sights and attractions are open year-round, although **peak seasons** vary by region. However, the North Rim of the Grand Canyon is closed from mid-October through mid-May. High season in Southern Arizona is the **winter** (Oct–Apr), when many visitors come to escape colder climates. January is typically the coldest month, with average high temperatures ranging from 43° F/6°C in Flagstaff to 66°F/19°C in Phoenix and 65°F/18°C in Tucson. Phoenix and Tucson areas have desert climates with an average elevation of 1,200ft.

Throughout Arizona, the **summer** months (May–Sept) see the highest temperatures; afternoon thundershowers are common. Daytime temperatures in summer average 104°F/40°C in Phoenix and in Tucson 100°F/38°C. Flagstaff is slightly cooler at 80°F/27°C.

Resorts are busiest in winter months, and during Christmas and **spring** holidays. Winter, when mosquitoes are tolerable and migratory birds are plentiful, is the best time to view wildlife in parks and reserves, although birding festivals are held throughout the year due to the plentiful amount of bird life. The **monsoon** (or rainy season) is generally June to September, with the greatest precipitation occurring in July and August. Be sure to bring a hat, insect repellant, sunglasses and sunscreen, and an umbrella.

Desert Climates

Desert climates are found in **Central and Southern Arizona**, including the metro areas of Tucson and Phoenix. The average elevation in desert climates is 1,200 ft.

Mountain Climates

Mountain climates are found primarily in **Northern and North-central Arizona**, including the

Average Seasonal Temperatures in Desert Climates				
	Jan	Apr	Jul	Oct
Avg. High	66°F/19°C	84°F/29°C	106°F/41°C	88°F/31°C
Avg. Low	41°F/5°C	55°F/13°C	81°F/27°C	61°F/16°C
Rainfall	0.6in	0.22in	0.1in	0.86in

Average Seasonal Temperatures in Mountain Climates				
	Jan	Apr	Jul	Oct
Avg. High	43°F/6°C	58°F/14°C	82°F/28°C	63°F/17°C
Avg. Low	16°F/-9°C	27°F/-3°C	50°F/10°C	31°F/-5°C
Rainfall	2.18in	1.29in	2.4in	1.93in

MUST KNOW

Sunset Crater Volcano National Monument

©Gwen Cannon/Michelin

Flagstaff and the Grand Canyon. The average elevation is 7,000ft.

KNOW BEFORE YOU GO
Useful Websites

www.arizonaguide.com – Official website of the Arizona Office of Tourism.

www.arizonascenicroads.com – Information and itineraries for 24 scenic drives in the state.

az.gov – Official website of the State of Arizona, featuring news, and travel information for visitors as well as government services.

www.azstateparks.com – Features, fees and reservation information for Arizona's state parks.

www.arizonaguide.com/things-to-do/native-cultures/tribes – Information about Arizona's Native American Tribes.

www.azdra.com – Website of the Dude Ranches Association.

www.azhla.com – Website of the Arizona Hotel and Lodging Association.

www.azrvparks.com – Information about Arizona RV Parks and campgrounds.

www.dot.state.az.us – Information from the Arizona Department of Transportation.

Tourism Offices

Local tourist offices listed below provide information free of charge on topics such as accommodations, shopping, entertainment, festivals and recreation. Many visitor centers exist throughout the state.

Northern Arizona

Grand Canyon National Park Service Visitor Center – South Rim at Mather Point. www.nps.gov/grca.

National Geographic Visitor Center-Grand Canyon/Tusayan – 450 AZ Hwy. 64, Grand Canyon, 86023. 928-638-2468, www.explorethecanyon.com.

Page/Lake Powell Tourism Bureau – 647-A Elm St., Page, 86040. 888-261-7243, www.pagelakepowell tourism.com.

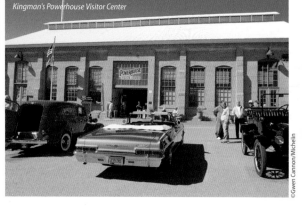

Kingman's Powerhouse Visitor Center

©Gwen Cannon/Michelin

Western Arizona

Kingman – Powerhouse Visitor Center – 120 W. Route 66, Kingman, 86401. 928-753-6106, www.kingmantourism.org.

Lake Havasu City Convention and Visitors Bureau – 314 London Bridge Rd., Lake Havasu City, 86403. 928-453-3444, www.golakehavasu.com.

Wickenburg Chamber of Commerce – 216 N. Frontier St., Wickenburg, 85390. 928-684-5479, www.wickenburgchamber.com.

Central Arizona

Flagstaff Visitor Center – 1 E. Route 66, Flagstaff, 86001. 928-774-9541, www.flagstaffarizona.org.

Jerome Chamber of Commerce – P. O. Box K, Jerome, 86331. 928-634-2900, www.jeromechamber.com.

Prescott Chamber of Commerce – 117 W. Goodwin St., Prescott, 86303. 928-445-2000, www.prescott.org.

Sedona Chamber of Commerce-Uptown Visitor Center – 331 Forest Rd., Sedona, 86339. 928-282-7722, www.sedonachamber.com.

Williams Chamber of Commerce – 200 Railroad Ave., Williams, 84046. 800-863-0546, www.experiencewilliams.com.

Phoenix Area

Phoenix Tourist Bureau – 400 E Van Buren St., Phoenix, 85004. 602-254-6500, www.visitphoenix.com.

Scottsdale Convention and Visitors Bureau – 4343 N. Scottsdale Rd., Suite 170, Scottsdale, 85251. 800-782-1117, www.experiencescottsdale.com.

Tucson and Southern Arizona

Metropolitan Tucson Tourist Bureau – 100 S. Church Ave., Tucson, 85701. 800-638-8350, www.visittucson.org.

City of Bisbee Visitor Center – 2 Copper Queen Plaza/Convention Center, Bisbee, 85603. 520-432-3554, www.discoverbisbee.com.

MUST KNOW

International Visitors

Foreign Embassies in North America

In addition to the tourism offices throughout Arizona, visitors from outside the US can obtain information from the US embassy or consulate in their country of residence (*partial listing below*). For a complete list of American consulates and embassies abroad, visit the US State Department Bureau of Consular Affairs listing online at: travel.state.gov. Many foreign countries have consular offices in Arizona (*for phone numbers, check the yellow pages of the telephone directory under Consulates*).

US Embassies Abroad

- **Belgium** – 27, boulevard du Régent, 1000 Brussels; 02 508-2111; belgium.usembassy.gov
- **Canada** – 490 Sussex Drive, Ottawa, Ontario K1N 1G8; 613-688-5335; canada.usembassy.gov
- **Germany** – Clayallee 170, 14191 Berlin; 30 238 3050; germany.usembassy.gov
- **Japan** – 10-5 Akasaka 1-Chome, Minato-ku Tokyo 107-8420; 03-3224-5000; tokyo.usembassy.gov
- **Switzerland** – Sulgeneckstrasse 19, 3007 Bern; 31 357 7011
- **United Kingdom** – 24 Grosvenor Square, London W1A 1AE; 207 499 9000

Entry Requirements

Citizens of countries participating in the Visa Waiver Pilot Program (VWPP) are not required to obtain a visa to enter the US for visits of fewer than 90 days if they have a machine-readable passport. Residents of visa-waiver countries must apply ahead for travel authorization online through the **ESTA program** (*www.cbp.gov/esta*). Travelers may apply any time before their travel; at least three days before departure is strongly recommended. Citizens of non-participating countries must have a visitor's visa. Upon entry, non-resident foreign visitors, including Canadians, must present a **valid passport** and round-trip transportation ticket. Naturalized Canadian citizens should carry their citizenship papers.

Air travelers between the US and Canada, Mexico, Central and South America, the Caribbean and Bermuda are also required to present a passport, Air NEXUS card or comparable documentation. All persons traveling between the US and destinations listed above, by land or by sea (including ferry), may be required to present a valid passport or other documentation, as determined by the US Dept. of Homeland Security. **Inoculations** are generally not required to enter the US, but check with the US embassy or consulate before departing.

Customs Regulations

All articles brought into the US must be declared at time of entry. **Items exempt** from customs regulations: personal effects; 150 milliliters (5 fl oz) of alcoholic beverage (providing visitor is at least 21 years old); 150 milliliters (5 fl oz) of perfume containing alcohol; 50 cigarettes and 10 cigars; and gifts (to persons in the US) that do not exceed $200 in value. **Prohibited items** include plant material, firearms and ammunition (if not intended for sporting purposes), and meat and poultry products. For other prohibited items, exemptions and information, contact the **US Customs Service**, 1300 Pennsylvania Ave. N.W., Washington DC 20229 (*202-354-1000; www.cbp.gov*).

Health

Before departing, visitors from abroad should check their health-care insurance to determine if doctors' visits, medication and hospitalization in the US are covered. Health care is not universal in the US, and though Europeans may receive emergency treatment, they cannot visit a doctor without travel insurance or prepayment of some sort. Prescription drugs should be properly identified, and accompanied by a copy of the prescription. Hotel staff can make recommendations for doctors and other medical services.

Companies offering **travel insurance** within the US include: **Access America** (*800-284-8300; www.accessamerica.com*); **Travelex** (*800-228-9792; www.travelex-insurance.com*); and **Travel Insured International** (*800-243-3174; www.travelinsured.com*).

Wildlife Safety

For those who hike, camp or fishing in Arizona, wildlife encounters are possible. Mountain lions, bobcats, rattlesnakes and even black bears might be present in certain areas. **Javelina**, or collared peccary, are found in Southern Arizona and north of Phoenix; these four-legged, pig-like creatures live in small herds and exist primarily on prickly pear cactus. Never feed wild animals. Try to avoid them altogether by altering your route; give them an opportunity to leave the area. For ways to discourage animal encounters, contact the Arizona Game and Fish Department (*www.azgfd.gov*). **Cacti** and other thorny plants are prevalent along trails and in campsites in desert climates; the spines of these plants can be painful if not cautiously avoided.

Practical Guide to Wildlife Encounters

For anyone out hiking, camping or fishing in the wild, wildlife encounters are possible. Bears, javelina, mountain lions, bobcats and rattlesnakes may frequent the areas you are in. Never feed or encourage these animals and at best try to avoid an encounter by altering your route. Give the animal a chance to leave the area. For ways to discourage animal encounters, contact the Arizona Game and Fish Department (www.azgfd.gov) before heading out on your adventure.

Cacti and other thorny plants exist in the desert climates along trails and in campsites. The spines of these plants can be painful and should be avoided. Rattlesnakes are reticent creatures and only coil to strike if they feel threatened. Be alert and watch where you walk or step when hiking and camping. If you find yourself near a snake, stop and stay still or back up slowly. Use common sense and watch your step. Be respectful of nature by following the rules of the trails, parks and camping areas.

GETTING THERE
By Air

Several US airlines offer direct and nonstop flights to Arizona via its international airports of **Phoenix Sky Harbor International** (*602-273-3300; www.skyharbor.com*); and **Tucson International** (*520-573-8100; www.flytucsonairport.com*). **McCarran International** in Las Vegas, Nevada (*702-261-5211; www.mccarran.com*), is 31mi from northwest Arizona. For flight information, contact the airline directly. Arizona's **regional airports** are usually accessible through commuter carriers.

By Train

The **Amtrak rail network** offers various train-travel packages that may combine rail, air and bus. Advance reservations are recommended. First-class, coach and sleeping cars are available; on some routes, two-level **Superliner** cars with floor-to-ceiling windows provide panoramic views. Canadian travelers should inquire with local travel agents regarding Amtrak/ VIARail connections.

The **USA RailPass** (*not available to US or Canadian citizens, or legal residents*) offers unlimited travel within Amtrak-designated regions at discounted rates: Passes are available in three travel durations and segments (15 days/8 segments, 30 days/12 segments, 45 days/ 18 segments) throughout the entire US.

By Car

Three major interstate highways connect other states to Arizona. From California, I-8 enters Arizona via Yuma running east-west and joins I-10 at Casa Grande.

Interstate-10 runs east-west through Southern Arizona and continues into New Mexico. Interstate-40 runs east-west across Northern Arizona.

By Bus

Greyhound offers access to major cities in Arizona (*800-752-4841, US only; www.greyhound.com*). The **Discovery Pass** allows unlimited travel anywhere for 7, 15, 30 or 60 days. Advance reservations are recommended. For fares, schedules and routes: 800-231-2222; www.discoverypass.com.

GETTING AROUND
By Car

Interstate-40 runs east-west across Northern Arizona with points of interest along the route: Petrified Forest National Park, Meteor Crater, Flagstaff and Winslow. Interstate-17 runs between Phoenix and Flagstaff with Montezuma Castle National Monument, the old mining town of Jerome and Red Rock Country near

©Gwen Cannon/Michelin

Phoenix Sky Harbor International Airport

Sedona as points of interest. I-17 connects I-40 with Interstate-10. Interstate-10 runs east-west through Southern Arizona connecting Phoenix to Tucson. Interstate-19 heads south from Tucson to Nogales, Mexico; along the way travellers can visit the old Mission San Xavier del Bac, Tubac Presidio State Park and Tumacácori National Historical Park.

Interstate-8 runs east-west between Yuma and Interstate-10 at Casa Grande. Two state parks and the Fortuna Foothills near Yuma are points of interest.

To get to the Grand Canyon, take I-40 to Highway 89 or 180. If you continue north on Highway 89, it will lead to the Glen Canyon National Recreational Area and Page, Arizona, which sits at the southern end of Lake Powell.

Rental Cars

Most large rental companies have offices at (or near) major airports and at downtown locations. Rentals typically include unlimited mileage. If a vehicle is returned at a different location from where it was rented, drop-off charges may be incurred. Reservations can be made online, or by calling a toll-free number, and giving your credit card information. Minimum age for rental is 25 years of age, but some car rental companies have special programs for 20 to 25 year olds.

Be sure to check for proper **insurance coverage**, offered at extra charge. Liability is not automatically included in the terms of the lease. Drivers are required to have personal-injury protection and property liability insurance; carry proof of insurance in the vehicle at all times.

Car Rental Companies

- ◆ **Alamo** – 800-327-9633 www.alamo.com.
- ◆ **Avis** – 800-331-1212 www.avis.com.
- ◆ **Budget** – 800-527-0700 www.budget.com.
- ◆ **Dollar** – 800-800-4000 www.dollar.com.
- ◆ **Enterprise**– 800-325-8007 www.enterprise.com.
- ◆ **Hertz** – 800-654-3131 www.hertz.com.
- ◆ **National** – 800-227-7368 www.nationalcar.com.
- ◆ **Thrifty** – 800-331-4200 www.thrifty.com.

(Toll-free numbers above are not accessible outside US.)

Recreational Vehicle (RV) Rentals

Motor-home rentals are offered from several locations in Arizona. Some models accommodate up to eight people, and service can include free mileage and airport transfers. Make reservations 2–3 weeks in advance. In the summer months (*Jun–Aug*) and during holiday seasons, reservations should be made at least 4–6 weeks in advance.

Contact **Cruise America RV Rentals**: 480-464-7300 or 800-671-8042; www.cruiseamerica.com.

Rules of the Road

The maximum **speed limit** on interstate highways is 75mph, and 65mph on state highways, unless otherwise posted. Speed limits are generally 25mph within city limits and residential areas. Distances are posted in miles (1 mile=1.6 kilometers).

Apart from local authorities, motor clubs (membership required) such

MUST KNOW

The Granite Dells, near Prescott

©Gwen Cannon/Michelin

as the **American Automobile Association (AAA)** *(800-222-4357; www.aaa.com)* offer roadside assistance:

The following are important rules:

◆ Drive on the right side of the road.
◆ Headlights must be turned on when driving in fog and rain.
◆ International visitors bearing valid driver's licenses issued by their country of residence are not required to obtain an International Driver's License in the US.
◆ **Seat belts** must be worn by all front-seat occupants.
◆ Right turns at a red light are allowed after coming to a complete stop, unless otherwise indicated.
◆ Children under 6 must ride in an approved child-safety seats (offered by most car-rental agencies; request these when making reservations).
◆ Motorists in both directions must come to a complete stop when warning signals on a **school bus** are activated.
◆ Do not drink and drive.

In Case of Accident

If you are involved in an accident resulting in personal injury or property damage, you must notify the local police and remain at the scene until dismissed. If blocking traffic, vehicles should be moved. In the case of property damage to an unattended vehicle, the driver must attempt to locate the owner or leave written notice in a conspicuous place of the driver's name, address and car registration number. If you carry a cell phone, **dial 911** if a major accident.

By Bus

Arizona's largest cities offer decent local bus service: it's usually inexpensive, and fairly easy to use. In some cities, the local bus lines service hotel zones and major attractions, making bus travel convenient, especially if parking for attractions must be paid for or is difficult to find.

By Taxi

Taxis are widely available in cities across Arizona. For more information: 1-800 TAXICAB, www.1800taxicab.com.

ACCESSIBILITY
Disabled Travelers

Many of the sights described in this guide are accessible to people with special needs. US Federal law requires that businesses, including hotels and restaurants, provide access for disabled people, devices for people who are hearing impaired, and designated parking spaces. Many public buses are equipped with wheelchair lifts and many hotels have rooms designed for disabled guests. For more information, contact the **Society for the Advancement of Travel and Hospitality (SATH)**, 347 Fifth Ave., Suite 610, New York NY 10016 *(212-447-7284; www.sath.org)*.

All **national parks** have facilities for disabled visitors. Free or discounted passes are available. For details, contact the National Park Service *(202-208-4747; www.nps.gov/pub_aff/access)*. For **state parks**, check with azstateparks.com. Passengers who will need assistance with **train** or **bus** travel should give advance notice to **Amtrak** *(800-872-7245 or 800-523-6590 (TDD); www.amtrak.com)* or **Greyhound** *(800-752-4841(US only) or 800-345-3109 (TDD); www.greyhound.com)*.

BASIC INFORMATION
Accommodations

For suggested lodgings and information about hotel rates and reservations, see Hotels. Although Arizona is a year-round destination, rates are lower in **off-season** (Jun–Sept in Southern Arizona). In some hotels children under 18 stay free when sharing a room with their parents. Some small hotel and many motel rooms include efficiency kitchens, and all but the most basic accommodations are air-conditioned. **Hotel taxes,** which vary according to location, range from 6 percent to 12.5 percent, and are not included in quoted rates. The *Arizona Official State Visitor's Guide* lists members of the Arizona Hotel & Lodging Association; the guide is available by calling 602-364-3700 or visiting www.arizonaguide.com.

Hotel Reservations

Rack rates (published rates) provided by hotels are usually higher than website deals. For more information, check with the local convention and visitors bureaus in the area you are visiting.

Hostels and Campsites

If you're traveling on a tight budget, consider staying at a hostel *(www.hostels.com)* or a campground. Dormitory-style **hostel** rooms average around $15–$40/night. Private rooms are available at additional charge, and amenities may include swimming pools, air-conditioning, common living room, laundry facilities, a self-service kitchen, dining room and Wi-Fi. Blankets and pillows are provided; linens can be rented. **Campsites** are located in national parks, state parks, national forests, and in private campgrounds. Many sites offer full utility hookups, lodges or cabins. Contact www.camparizona.com or koa.com/states-provinces.

Discounts

Students, children and senior citizens often get discounts at attractions and hotels. Many establishments offer discounts

MUST KNOW

to persons over age 62, including members of the **American Association of Retired Persons (AARP)** (*601 E St. N.W., Washington, DC, 20049; 888-687-2277; www. aarp.org*).

Business Hours
Banks
Banks are generally open Mon–Thu 9am–4:30pm, and Fri until 5pm or 6pm. Some banks in larger cities may be open Saturday morning until noon. Most **state and federal government** buildings (including city halls) are open Mon–Fri 8:30am–4:30pm. Most banks and government offices are closed on major holidays.

Attractions
Hours for individual attractions are given in each entry. Closing dates vary; note that most sights and attractions are closed Thanksgiving Day and Dec 25, and many are closed on major holidays (when government offices are closed).

Shops
As a rule, malls and shopping centers are open Mon–Sat 10am–9pm, and Sun noon–6pm.

Pharmacies
Pharmacies are generally open Mon–Fri 8am–10pm, Sat 9am–9pm, and Sun 10am–6pm. Many CVS and Walgreens pharmacies are open 24 hours. Go online, check the Yellow Pages phone directory or ask at your hotel.

Electricity
Electrical current in the US is 120 volts AC, 60 Hz. Foreign-made appliances may need voltage transformers and North American flat-blade adapter plugs (available at specialty travel and electronics stores).

Internet
The Internet is widely available in hotels, Wi-Fi hot spots, public libraries and internet cafes throughout Arizona.

Liquor Laws
The legal minimum age for purchase and consumption of alcoholic beverages is 21; proof of age is required. Liquor is sold in liquor stores only, while beer and wine are available at grocery stores. Consuming liquor in public places and carrying an open liquor

©Gwen Cannon/Michelin

Mather Campground, Grand Canyon National Park

container in a moving vehicle is illegal.

Mail

Letters can be mailed from most hotels as well as from post offices. Stamps and packing material may be purchased at post offices, grocery stores and businesses offering postal and express-shipping services located throughout the state *(search online or see the Yellow Pages phone directory under "Mailing Services")*. Most post offices are open Mon–Fri 9am–5pm, some are also open Sat 9am–noon.

Money/Currency

Currency is the US Dollar and comes in notes of $1, $5, $10, $20, $50 and $100. Coins come in denominations of 1, 5, 10 and 25 cents, as well as one dollar.

Banks

Most banks are members of the network of Automated Teller Machines (ATM), allowing visitors from around the world to withdraw cash using bank cards and major credit cards. ATMs can usually be found in airports, banks, grocery stores and shopping malls.

Credit Cards

All major credit cards are accepted in hotels, most restaurants, stores, entertainment venues and gas stations in Arizona. To report a lost or stolen **credit card**:

* **American Express** –
  800-528-4800
* **Diners Club Card** –
  800-234-6377
* **Master Card** – 800-627-8372
* **Visa** – 800-947-2911

Traveler's Checks

Most banks will cash brand-name traveler's checks only with proper identification, and process cash advances on major credit cards with proper identification. The traveler's checks of registered guests are generally accepted by hotels. But more and more stores and restaurants do not accept them. **American Express Company Travel Service** (*www. americanexpress.com*) has offices in Phoenix.

Currency Exchange

Currency can be exchanged at most banks (fee applies). Currency-exchange services are also available at the international airport in Phoenix; there is an ATM currency exchange in Tucson International Airport.

Smoking

Smoking is banned in most enclosed indoor workplaces and public spaces, including restaurants, in Arizona.

Taxes

Prices displayed or quoted in the US do not generally include State **sales tax** (6.6 percent in Arizona). Sales tax is added at the time of purchase and is not reimbursable (it can sometimes be avoided if purchased items are shipped to another country by the seller). The hotel occupancy tax and tax rate for rental cars vary according to location; daily surcharges may be added as well. Some counties levy an additional local sales tax (4 percent), and/or a 1 percent to 5 percent tourist tax.

MUST KNOW

Tipping

In the US it is customary to give money for services rendered by waitstaff, porters, hotel maids and taxi drivers. In restaurants, patrons normally tip the server 15 percent to 20 percent of the bill. (In popular tourist locations restaurants may automatically add a **service charge**; check your bill before you leave a tip). At hotels, porters are generally given $1 per suitcase, housekeeping staff $1 per day. Taxi drivers are usually tipped 15 percent of the fare.

Telephones

Some public telephones accept credit cards, and all will accept long-distance calling cards. For **long-distance calls** in the US and Canada, dial 1 + area code (3 digits) + number (7 digits). To place a **local call**, dial the 7-digit number without 1 or the area code (unless the local calling area includes several area codes). To find a **long-distance** number, dial 1 + area code + 555-1212 *(there is a charge for this service)*. For operator assistance or information, dial **0** for the local operator or **00** for the long-distance operator. To place an **international call**, dial **011** + country code + area code + number. A list of country and city codes can be found in

the beginning of local phone directories. To place a collect call (person receiving the call pays charges), dial **0** + area code + number and tell the operator you are calling collect. If it is an international call, ask for the overseas operator.

Most telephone numbers in this guide that start with **800** or **888** or **877** are toll-free (no charge) in the US and may not be accessible outside North America. Dial **1** before dialing a toll-free number. Most hotels add a **surcharge** for both local and long-distance calls.

Temperature and Measurement

In the US temperatures are measured in degrees Fahrenheit and measurements are expressed according to the US Customary System of weights and measures.

Time Zone

Arizona is in the Mountain Time Zone and does not observe Daylight Saving Time except in the Navajo Indian Reservation.

Know What Time It Is?

The sun rises and sets at almost the same moment in Zion, Utah, and Flagstaff, Arizona, as well as in Window Rock, Arizona and Gallup, NM. But in all these places, clocks don't always show the same time. This chronological Tower of Babel is the result of disparate political attitudes about Daylight Saving Time (DST). Arizona doesn't observe it—but most of the rest of the country does. Further complicating matters is the fact that the Navajo Nation does observe DST—and the Hopi Nation, which is entirely contained within the Navajo reservation, does not observe DST, like Arizona.

SOUTHWEST'S HEART

Anchoring the Southwestern United States, both geographically and metaphysically, America's sixth-largest state spreads out over 113,909sq mi, much of it scrub desert. Neighboring Arizona on four sides are the states of Utah to the north, New Mexico to the east, Nevada and California on its west, plus the country of Mexico along its southern border. Arizona's greatest landmark is the vast and beautiful Grand Canyon, slicing through the state's northern reaches. A number of Indian reservations occupy large swathes of terrain within the state. Once the heart of the Western frontier, Arizona was a late admission to the Union, in 1912 (number 48), but has since grown to be one of the most populous of the 50 states, ranking 16th, with 6 million.

Dubbed the "Valley of the Sun," Arizona's winterless capital, **Phoenix**, represents the nation's 14th-largest urban area, with 4.3 million residents. Until the recession of 2008, the city was among the country's fastest-growing US metro areas. Though largely seen in the public imagination as cactus-strewn desert, Arizona stretches from riparian streamside less than 100 feet in elevation, along the **Colorado River** near Yuma, to the snowy alpine heights of 12,633ft **Humphreys Peak** near Flagstaff. It is the only state that contains portions of all four major US deserts, the Sonoran, Mojave, Chihuahuan and Great Basin; but it also has thousands of square miles of pine uplands that hold three ski areas. It includes almost half the 1,400mi length of the Rocky Mountain-born Colorado River, which not only formed the **Grand Canyon**, but brings the state billions of gallons of water that enabled its 20C boom. The river forms much of Arizona's western border with California.

Arizona is firmly fixed in the human imagination as a vast land of towering **saguaros**, frontier history, baking sun and what may be earth's best-known landscape feature, the mile-deep, 277mi-long Grand Canyon. Though John Ford made northern Arizona's **Monument Valley** a living film set for movies such as *Stagecoach*, Southern Arizona is the cradle of events that turned history into legend. Here, Apache leaders **Cochise** and **Geronimo** fought against American control as late as 1886—the last Indian warriors were not relieved of "prisoner of war" status until 1913. The West's most famous (and still controversial) gunfight took

Fast Facts

Statehood: 1912 (48th state in the Union)

Area: 113,909sq mi; 6th-largest US state

Population: 6,482,505 (2011)

Largest city: Phoenix

Capital: Phoenix

Highest point: Humphreys Peak, 12,637ft

Major industries: agriculture, tourism, defense, mining, real estate

Rattlesnake species: 11

The Meaning of "Arizona"

In a state where no one can say for sure if the most fabled lost mine of all even exists, it's appropriate that no one is certain where the name "Arizona" originated. Is it a corruption of a Native name, *Aleh-zon*, that meant place with a small spring? Is it a Spanish version of an Aztec word, *arizuma*, that meant "silver-bearing"? Or does it derive from a Basque word that means "good oak tree"? Arizona's state historian leans to the latter meaning, which corresponds to a name given an early Spanish ranchería.

place at **Tombstone's OK Corral** in 1881, cementing Wyatt Earp's name in frontier folklore. The **Lost Dutchman Gold Mine** was first rumored to lie hidden in the Superstition Mountains east of Phoenix in 1892, and tens of thousands of hardy adventurers have sought it ever since. To this day, no one knows exactly what happened at the OK Corral; or whether the Lost Dutchman exists at all. But 37 million tourists visit Arizona each year in search of modern gold: reliable winter sun and warmth, a bracing view into the Grand Canyon, and encounters with Western history and **Native American culture**.

The landscape of Arizona includes rock as old as 2 billion years; exposed to the air at the bottom of the Grand Canyon, most of whose exposed layers represent sediments from long-ago seas. Carved by the Colorado and Salt rivers, and tucked between weather-blocking mountain ranges—the coastal ranges of California and the Rocky Mountains eastward—the state is largely arid, with **annual precipitation** ranging from just over 3 inches at Yuma to roughly 30 inches on Humphreys Peak. The **Sonoran Desert** encompasses much of Southern Arizona; the **Mojave Desert** mantles far Western Arizona; the Great Basin desert dips into Northwest Arizona; and the Chihuahuan tips a tiny finger into the southeastern part of the state. Within Arizona, all four deserts are known for the **summer monsoon** phenomenon, when moist subtropical air boils

Phoenix skyline

©Jill Richards, 2008/Greater Phoenix CVB

north from the Pacific Ocean to create massive thunderstorms that, while infrequent, unleash torrents of localized rain. **Flash floods** are an almost-daily occurrence somewhere in Arizona during the monsoon season, which typically runs from late June to early September.

This periodic resupply of water stores is what made the region habitable to its original settlers, the first of whom appeared roughly 12,000 years ago. The **aboriginal inhabitants** survived as hunter-gatherers until agriculture made its way north from Mexico in the early part of the first millennium AD; corn, beans, squash and other Central American crops led to the development of a cliff-dwelling civilization in the northern part of the state. These **Ancestral Puebloan** peoples were adept masons and basket-weavers; meanwhile, indigenous peoples in Southern Arizona such as the **Hohokam** built sophisticated irrigation systems to support valley-bottom villages. Two new peoples of Athabaskan origin, the

Grand Canyon, Navajo Hogan 1913

©U.S. Geological Survey

Navajo and **Apache**, arrived from the far north in the early part of the second millennium.

When Spanish explorers arrived in 1539, their quest was simple but fruitless—gold. Franciscan and Jesuit friars followed, seeking a different treasure: unclaimed souls. The mission at **San Xavier del Bac**, south of present-day **Tucson**, was founded in 1692; the 1780s church at its site is the oldest European building in Arizona.

A few silver strikes in the region brought new **Spanish settlers** and prospectors, but the territory was far off the global radar until US armies marched across it during the **Mexican-American War** of 1846. In 1850 most of the region was absorbed into the Territory of New Mexico; the 1853 **Gadsden Purchase** added a strip along the southern border to form Arizona's present-day scope.

A small silver boom around **Tubac** in 1856 brought more settlers, and Arizona became its own territory in 1864. Further gold and copper discoveries fueled growth; **Bisbee** became a boom town. Arizona was little touched by the Civil War, but persistent conflict with Apaches in the south led to some of the most famous campaigns of the Indian wars. These conflicts largely ended with the final surrender of Geronimo in September 1886—though Apache raiders struck into Arizona from Mexico as late as 1917. Meanwhile, northern Arizona's **Navajo** people transformed America's largest Indian reservation into an autonomous nation within three states.

In the early 20C, the territory's **economy** was based on cattle,

🐾 Wild in the Desert

Arizona is one of the best states to see wild animals. California condors, hawks and eagles (both bald and golden) soar in the skies above the Grand Canyon. Deer are omnipresent in the pine woodlands of northern Arizona. Falcons and other raptors ply the lowlands and open country. However, the Sonoran Desert of Southern Arizona is ideal for wildlife viewing. Javelinas, North America's only native pigs, abound; a dozen kinds of rattlesnakes prowl the scrub-brush; bobcats and coyotes stalk the numerous rabbits; the rare Gila monster scuttles along in the sand. Most of these creatures are often seen in the urban-fringed foothills of the mountains around Phoenix and especially, Tucson. Foothills hiking trails are the best place to look for them. (None are dangerous unless one actively molests them.)

Here, too, are found more hummingbirds than anywhere else in the US, especially in two preserves southeast of Tucson, Ramsey Canyon and Madera Canyon. Up to two dozen types of hummers may be found here in the winter, including rare sorts that wander north from Mexico, and hikers are invariably rewarded by the spectacle of these avian jewels dashing about at midday. For more information visit www.nature.org or www.friendsofmaderacanyon.org.

copper and cotton; the population had risen above 200,000 upon statehood in 1912. The first big public irrigation system, the **Salt River Project**, began fueling farm and population growth in the 1920s; the massive **Central Arizona Project** added millions of acre-feet of water from the Colorado River in the 1980s. Meanwhile, **tourism** began as Americans started seeking warm, dry climates for health sojourns in Tucson and **Scottsdale**. The invention of air-conditioning in the mid-20C opened the state to a boom in residential and travel growth, and the population doubled fivefold between 1960 and 2000. Residential development surged until the real estate collapse of 2008; at one point during the consequent slump, one in every seven houses in the Phoenix metro area was vacant. Today Arizona's economy is a diverse array of technology, agriculture, defense and tourism. The latter industry draws millions to lavish resorts in the Phoenix area and Tucson, where visitors relax in the sun, pamper themselves in famed spas, play golf on hundreds of sun-splashed courses, and retreat to **guest ranches** for horseback riding. Within these resort centers, it can be hard to remember that this is, after all, a desert state whose landscape holds raw natural wonders such as the Grand Canyon. And then—even in the heart of Phoenix—one catches sight of a stately saguaro, illuminated by a red desert sky, and Arizona's true nature asserts itself. Though there may be a sparkling swimming pool nearby, it's clear that both sides of the state's modern character hold the treasure Spanish adventurers hoped to find four centuries ago.

GRAND CANYON★★★

Encompassing almost one-fifth of Arizona, the region north of I-40 and west of Flagstaff is a high-desert plateau, creased by what may be the best-known topographical feature on earth, the Grand Canyon. Occupying the northwest part of the state, this 277mi-long chasm averages 10mi wide and 1mi deep. It lays bare rocks dating back almost 2 billion years, and draws millions of visitors a year to gawk at its depths and multi-hued layers. It is by far the most significant attraction in the region—but not the only one by any means. Just across the border in Utah lie other famous canyonlands whose unique stone monoliths and vivid colors star in a thousand photographs.

The Grand Canyon has been inhabited for at least 4,000 years; artifacts of the Desert Archaic culture have been found in niches in the canyon walls. By 500 AD, the Ancestral Puebloan culture was established. The earliest European visit was by Francisco Vásquez de Coronado's gold-hungry 1540 expedition. In 1869 a one-armed Civil War veteran named **John Wesley Powell** led an expedition of nine men in small wooden boats down the canyon. Late-19C mining efforts generally failed, but opened the doors for tourism. The first rim-top hotels were little more than mining camps. floor. In 1919 was the National Park was established.

GRAND CANYON NATIONAL PARK★★★

$25/vehicle (7-day pass).
Open daily year-round, except for weather-related road closures.
928-638-7888. www.nps.gov/grca.

Stretching 277mi in length and averaging 10mi wide and 1mi deep, the Grand Canyon is nothing short of magnificent. No other place has so much of the earth's geological history on display, or presents such a memorable sight. Most visitor services are centered on the canyon's **South Rim**. The less commercialized **North Rim** can be explored mid-May through mid-October. Beyond that, the

North Rim, Grand Canyon

©Leslie Forsberg/Michelin

Practical Information

When to Go

May and June are the finest months weather-wise at the South Rim. July and August are the peak of **monsoon** season in Arizona, with almost daily thunderstorms. Crowds and rain diminish toward the end of August. September and October bring cooler weather. The South Rim remains open through the winter, but is cold: temperatures below zero have been recorded November to March. The North Rim is always less crowded and cooler than the South; snow and lack of visitors **close the access road** mid-October through mid-May.

Getting There

◆ **By Car** – Grand Canyon Village on the South Rim is accessible 79mi north of Flagstaff via US 180 and Rte. 64. A more scenic route is 109mi north from Flagstaff on US 89 and Rte. 64. A third route is Rte. 64 north of Williams 60mi. The North Rim lies 208mi north of Flagstaff via US89/89A and Rte. 67, and 278mi east of Las Vegas along I-15, then Rtes. 59, 389 and 67.

◆ **By Train** – **Grand Canyon Railway** (see below) offers daily service between Williams and Grand Canyon Village, eliminating parking at the oft-crowded South Rim.

◆ **By Bus** – Tour companies offer bus trips from Flagstaff, Phoenix and Las Vegas to the canyon. Except in the case of Flagstaff, these journeys can be day-long or overnight trips; the latter includes lodging at the canyon rim. Las Vegas tour companies also offer one-day trips (15hrs) to the North Rim, most notably **Grand Canyon Tour Co.** (705-655-6060 or 800-222-6966; www.grandcanyontours.com).

Getting Around

◆ **By Car** – Vehicles are permitted on the park's main road, but not permitted on Hermit Road and Yaki Point Road (free shuttle buses operate on these roads). **Parking**: Park only in designated areas. Do not park along the road, except where signs indicate parking is permissible. The large lots nearest the Visitor Center at Grand Canyon Village on the South Rim fill up early in summer.

◆ **By Bus** – **Trans-Canyon Shuttle** operates daily bus service between the two rims mid-May to mid-Oct; southbound in the morning, northbound in the evening. Each trip takes 4.5hrs. Reservations are required ($85; 928-638-2820; www.trans-canyonshuttle.com).

◆ **By Shuttle** – The park operates four different shuttle buses, all free, plying various routes in Grand Canyon Village and along the West Rim to Hermits Rest. Major hotels, the airport, the train depot and key sights within the area are easily reached using the buses.

Visitor Information

The main visitor center is in Grand Canyon Village at **Mather Point** (928-638-7888; www.nps.gov/grca) where you can obtain free **maps** of the park as well as literature about lodgings, hiking trails and other information. Exhibits focus on canyon history, geology, flora and fauna. Rangers are on hand to answer questions.

Accommodations

Many visitors spend more than one day at the canyon. Several historic lodges and cabins offer overnight accommodations, as well as dining, in the park.

Reservations

For reservations for South Rim lodgings listed below contact **Xanterra** (303-297-2757 or 888-297-2757; www.grandcanyonlodges. com). To reserve Grand Canyon Lodge (closed in winter), contact **Forever Resorts** (877-386-4383; foreverlodging.com/lodging). Six-months to one-year advance reservations are strongly advised.

Prices

Rates vary from year to year. Prices shown reflect the average cost for a standard double room for two people, not including taxes, tips or surcharges.

$$$	$175-$250
$$	$100-$175
$	under $100

SOUTH RIM

El Tovar Hotel
$$$ 78 rooms

The historic hotel that anchors the village lodging complex next to the train depot was built in 1905 by the Fred Harvey Company long before the canyon received park designation. Remodeled many times over the years (most recently in 2005), it is one of the oldest and most atmospheric national park lodges in the country. Its "rustic luxury" design by Charles Whittlesey features local stone and Oregon pine. The eclectic interior marries Mission, Arts-and-Crafts and Swiss Alps furnishing styles. Its walls lie just 20ft from the canyon rim. A meal in the dining room is a treat—plenty of waitstaff as well as canyon views.

♦ Kachina/Thunderbird Lodges
$$$ 104 rooms

This pair of modern, two-level lodges neighbors El Tovar and Bright Angel Lodge. About half of the rooms permit views of the canyon, but their rates are slightly higher. Rooms are fairly spacious and furnished with two queens or a king bed and have a full bath.

♦ Yavapai Lodge
$$ 358 rooms

Located in a forested area about a half mile from the canyon's edge, this lodge is the park's largest. Of the two buildings, Yavapai East has the majority of rooms, all of which are air-conditioned; the rooms in West are not, but have ceiling fans. The cafe serves three meals a day. Next door to the lodge are a general store, bank and post office.

♦ Bright Angel Lodge
$-$$ 39 rooms, 50 cabins

The same company that runs El Tovar operates five other lodges in the village, including the historic Bright Angel Lodge. Designed by Mary Colter, famed architect for Fred Harvey, it opened in 1935. Its fireplace famously features rocks representing all the geologic layers found in the canyon below. Take a peek at memorabilia about Colter and the Harvey Girls in the **History Room**, where an original touring carriage is on display. Southwest fare is served in the dining room.

♦ Maswik Lodge
$ 278 rooms

Housed in two buildings (Maswik North and Maswik South), this contemporary lodge, rustic in appearance, sits among pine trees a quarter-mile from the canyon rim. Motel-type rooms come equipped with two queen beds and a private bath. A cafeteria is on-site. Cabins are available in the summer.

CANYON FLOOR

♦ Phantom Ranch
$-$$ 4 dorms, 11 cabins
Edging Bright Angel Creek on the canyon floor, this rustic ranch is open year-round. Designed by Mary Colter and opened in 1922, it was built of native stone and wood. Accessed only by foot, mule or the Colorado River, and booked primarily by hikers, rafters and mule-tour participants, it is a very popular place to overnight (advance reservations are highly recommended). Cabins (for 4 people) and dormitories (separate quarters for women and men; 10 bunk beds per dorm) are equipped with bunk beds and include bedding. Bathrooms are shared. Meals served in the canteen must be reserved in advance, preferably at the time of room reservations.

NORTH RIM

♦ Grand Canyon Lodge
$$-$$$ 40 rooms, 179 cabins
877-386-4383. foreverlodging.com/lodging. Closed mid-Oct–mid-May.
The heart of North Rim's visitor complex is this historic lodge, originally opened in 1928 and rebuilt in 1937 after a fire, both times under the purview of architect Gilbert Stanley Underwood. Constructed in local Kaibab limestone, the building perches right on the rim. The interior features a priceless collection of early 20C Navajo rugs, including one hanging above the lobby that is one of the largest ever made. Two verandas overlook the canyon—one with a fireplace. Accommodations range from a few deluxe rim-side cottages to bunk-style rustic cabins (all with a bathroom) to motel-style rooms with a queen bed and private bath.

largely undeveloped Arizona Strip lies just south of the Utah border. Though separated by just 10mi as the crow flies, the South Rim and North Rim are more than 200 road miles apart. The drive from rim to rim takes a 4-5 hours. Many visitors opt for a shorter hop to Williams *(60mi south)*, terminus for the Grand Canyon Railway *(see below)*. Ancestral Puebloan people have lived in the area for centuries. About 2,000 Ancestral Puebloan sites, including **petroglyphs**, have been found within park boundaries; most impressive is the **Tusayan Pueblo** (c.1185) on the South Rim.

Much credit for developing the park for visitation goes to the **Fred Harvey Company**, which built

Touring Tip

The most scenic and least commercial route into the canyon is from its east side via Route 64 from **Cameron** *(at US 89)* to the East Rim and then east to Grand Canyon Village. The dramatic landscape along this 50mi stretch gradually reveals smaller canyons that preview the gigantic chasm that's to come.

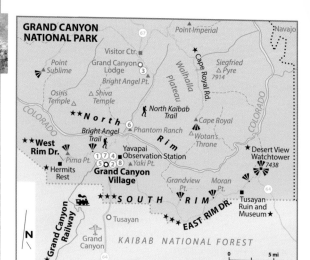

GRAND CANYON NATIONAL PARK

Point Imperial · Navajo

Visitor Ctr.
Point Sublime
Grand Canyon Lodge ③
Bright Angel Pt.
Cape Royal Rd.
Siegfried Pyre 7914
Walhalla Plateau
Osiris Temple
Shiva Temple
★★ **North**
North Kaibab Trail
Cape Royal
Phantom Ranch
Wotan's Throne
Bright Angel Trail
★★ **West Rim Dr.**
Pima Pt.
① ⑦ ④
⑤ ⑤ ② ⑧
Yavapai Observation Station
Yaki Pt.
Grand Canyon Village
Desert View Watchtower 7438
Hermits Rest
Grandview Pt.
Moran Pt.
★★★ **SOUTH   RIM**
Tusayan Ruin and Museum ★
Grand Canyon Railway
Tusayan
★★★ **EAST RIM DR.**
Grand Canyon
KAIBAB   NATIONAL   FOREST

N

0 ____ 5 mi
0 ____ 10 km

HOTELS			
Bright Angel Lodge	①	Maswik Lodge	⑤
El Tovar Hotel	②	Phantom Ranch	⑥
Grand Canyon Lodge	③	Thunderbird Lodge	⑦
Kachina Lodge	④	Yavapai Lodge	⑧

railroad hotels and restaurants throughout the Southwest. Tourism began in earnest with the 1905 completion of the **El Tovar Hotel**. Designer Mary Colter conceived many of the Harvey buildings, including the canyon-floor **Phantom Ranch** (1922), and the **Bright Angel Lodge** (1935). Most were staffed by "Harvey Girls,"

Cameron Trading Post

1mi north of junction of US 89 and Rte. 64, in Cameron. 877-221-0690. www.camerontradingpost.com.

This large complex sitting near a suspension bridge over the **Little Colorado River** is a worthy stop in the middle of a dusty nowhere. The original 1916 **trading post** is now neighbored by a mammoth retail store, stocked to the rafters with apparel, jewelry, Native American wares, Western gear, and other gift items. At the back of the store, a large, pleasant **restaurant** with picture windows serves up stews, chili, tacos and Navajo fry bread at reasonable prices. The adjacent gallery displays exquisite, but pricey, Native American baskets, blankets, beadwork, pottery and katsina dolls. A **garden** outside the rear of the restaurant offers an oasis of greenery.

A Truly Grand Canyon

The Grand Canyon is not the world's deepest canyon. In North America alone, there are deeper chasms in Mexico (Copper Canyon), California (Kings Canyon) and the Pacific Northwest (Hells Canyon). Older rocks may be found in northern Canada and elsewhere. Nor is this the most popular US national park—that honor belongs to Great Smoky Mountains, with 9 million visitors a year. But the Grand Canyon is known throughout the world for its spectacular landscape and its special, almost mystical characteristics. At dawn and dusk, the low-angle sun highlights the vividly colored canyon walls. Bands of green, blue, purple, pink, red, orange, gold, yellow and white define a succession of exposed ancient rock layers. It is one of the most extreme cases of erosion anywhere, and a site where visitors feel humbled by the relentless, artistic power of nature. It's worth the walk to one of the less-crowded viewpoints to quietly experience the sense of infinity the canyon engenders.

well-dressed and educated young women, usually from the East; the "Girls" are gone, but the lodges continue to serve visitors.

In its first year as a national park, 44,000 people visited the Grand Canyon. Today, more than 4 million tourists enter the park each year. Their impact on the fragile environment has led the National Park Service to plan dramatic action to protect the canyon for future generations, and to establish a model that likely will be adapted at other US national parks. For instance, shuttle buses carry visitors during peak travel months to reduce traffic pollution; and water is no longer sold in plastic bottles within the park, thus sparing many tons of greenhouse gas emissions and preventing litter.

East Rim Drive★★★

The 24mi road from the East Rim Entrance Station to Grand Canyon Village passes numerous dizzying viewpoints, including Moran, Grandview, Lipan and Yaki Points.

The first viewpoint encountered, the **Desert View Watchtower★**, may be the most photographed structure in the park. Modeled after an ancient Pueblo lookout, the three-story construction is dominated by a circular 70ft tower that commands expansive **views★★★** of the convoluted canyon and Colorado River far below. The Painted Desert appears on the far eastern horizon.

A small pueblo ruin marks the **Tusayan Ruin and Museum★**, 4mi west of the entrance. Displays trace

©Gwen Cannon/Michelin
Desert View Watchtower

Tusayan Ruin and Museum

©Gwen Cannon/Michelin

the pre-13C culture of Ancestral Puebloans in the Grand Canyon region.

South Rim★★★

Most visitor activities in the park are focused along a 35mi strand of paved road that extends from the East Rim Entrance Station *(29mi west of US-89 at Cameron)* to Hermits Rest. **Grand Canyon Village** is the site of park headquarters, the main visitor center and the lion's share of historic hotels, restaurants and tourist facilities within the park.

Grand Canyon Village Historical District★

The district comprises nine buildings, including the El Tovar Hotel, **Hopi House**, Bright Angel Lodge and Lookout Studio. Trains from Williams still arrive at the **Santa Fe Railway Station** designed in 1909 by Francis Wilson.

Grand Canyon Railway★

In Grand Canyon Village, depot is across the road from El Tovar. Depot in Williams at 233 N. Grand Canyon Blvd.,65mi south of South Rim. 303-843-8724 or 800-843-8724. www.thetrain.com.
The Atchison-Topeka-Santa Fe Railroad operated between **Williams** and the canyon from 1901 to 1968; service was re-established in 1989. The 65mi one-way trip takes 2hrs15min, and is enlivened by strolling musicians and the somewhat hokey antics of Wild West characters on board.

Kolb Brothers Studio

Perched on the rim, west of the Bright Angel Lodge, the former studio (1904) now houses a bookstore and gallery. The two brothers photographed tourists descending by mule into the canyon, processed the film at Indian Garden, 4.5mi (by trail) and 4,000ft below the rim, and one would run back uphill to sell the photos to returning visitors.

Yavapai Observation Station

A mile east of the visitor center, this station acts as a sort of geology museum. Exhibits focus on the Grand Canyon's fossil record; guided geology walks depart several times daily.
The **Rim Trail** *(9.4mi)* extends gently west from here to Hermits

Rest; its first 2.7mi (to Maricopa Point) are paved and highly accessible.

West Rim Drive (Hermit Road)★★

Between March and November, only free shuttle buses ply this 7mi road west from Grand Canyon Village. The drive passes **viewpoints★★★** at Maricopa Point, the John Wesley Powell Memorial, Hopi Point, Mohave Point and Pima Point before ending at **Hermits Rest★**, named for a 19C prospector, loner Louis Boucher.

North Rim★★

Accessible from South Rim via Rte. 64 east to Cameron, US-89 north to Marble Canyon, US-89A west to Jacob Lake, then Rte. 67 south. Open mid-May–mid-Oct.

The North Rim is far less developed than the South Rim. At 7,700-8,800ft above sea level, the North Rim is about 1,200ft higher than the South Rim. It is also several degrees cooler, with midsummer temperatures averaging in the high-70s°F rather than mid-80s°F.

To many visitors, the North Rim offers a connoisseur's experience of the Grand Canyon. It is definitely less crowded, and the surrounding Kaibab Plateau is more visually appealing than the approach to the South Rim.

The North Rim **visitor center**, adjacent to Grand Canyon Lodge, is a good place to get one's bearings. A paved .5mi trail leads from it to **Bright Angel Point**, which affords glorious **views★★★** of the canyon. Also visible is the strenuous **North Kaibab Trail** (14.2mi), which descends 5,840ft to Phantom Ranch. Day hikers should not venture beyond Roaring Springs (*4.7mi each way*), the water source for the entire national park. Full- and half-day **mule trips** (*see The Great Outdoors*) are available from the North Rim, but do not descend all the way to the river. *These trips are highly unsuitable for anyone with a fear of heights.* **Cape Royal Road★** extends 23mi from the lodge southeast across the Walhalla Plateau to Vista Encantadora and Cape Royal, with a spur route to Point Imperial, the highest point on the canyon rim at 8,803ft.

Williams Depot, Grand Canyon Railway

©Gwen Cannon/Michelin

GRAND CANYON REGION

0 — 20 mi
0 — 50 km

N

RICHF

Modena

Frontier Homestead SP

Parowan   Pangu

143

15

Cedar City

Cedar Breaks NM

★★★ **BRYCE CANYON NP**

14

Cannony

Beaver Dam SP

18

Veyo

89

★★★ **ZION NP**

Glendale

89

Mt. Carmel Jct

St. George

Springdale

Quail Creek SP

Coral Pink Sand Dunes

Kanab.

N E V A D A

Colorado City

Kaibab

Fredonia

389

Pipe Spring NM

Jacob Lake

Desert NWR

188

Glendale

15

169

Moapa River

Logandale Overton

Valley of Fire

V I R G I N   W A S H   C L I F F S

Virgin

A R I Z O N A

KAIBAB NF

LAS VEGAS ★★★

LAKE MEAD

★ *LAKE MEAD NRA*

★★★ ***GRAND CANYO NATL. PARK***

GRAND CANYON-PARASHANT NM

Waterfalls

Hualapai Hilltop

Havasupai

●Supai   Nor

Grand Canyon Village

Boulder City

HOOVER DAM ★★★

Nelson

165

G R A N D

★★ **Skywalk**

Colorado

Diamond Creek

18

★★★ *SOUT*

93

LAKE MEAD NRA ★

Colorado

Hualapai

Peach Springs

66

Vale

★ **Grand Canyon Railway**

66

Seligman

Ash Fork

Laughlin   Bullhead City

★ **Kingman**

68

40

40

Willia

163

95

Mohave Valley

Havasu NWR

93

★★★ ***RED ROC COUNTR***

PRESCOTT NF

★ **Tuzigoot NM**

Needles

Chemehuevi

95

★ ○**Wikieup**

97

Chino Valley

Clarkdale

★ **Jerom**

CALIFORNIA

95

Lake Havasu City

▲*Cattail Cove SP*

Prescott

18

96

89

69

Vidal Jct.

Bill Williams River NWR ★

▲ *Alamo Lake SP*

○**Wickenburg** ★

PRESCOTT NF

62

Parker

Colorado River

95

72

Yarnell

71

Aguila

New River

74

Blythe

10

Quartzite

Hope

60

A R I Z O N A

Morristown

Sun City

101

95

Colorado

Yuma Proving Ground

KOFA NWR

Tonopah

Glendale

Gila

85

★★ **PHOENIX**

78

Cibola NWR

Joshua Forest Parkway

Gila River

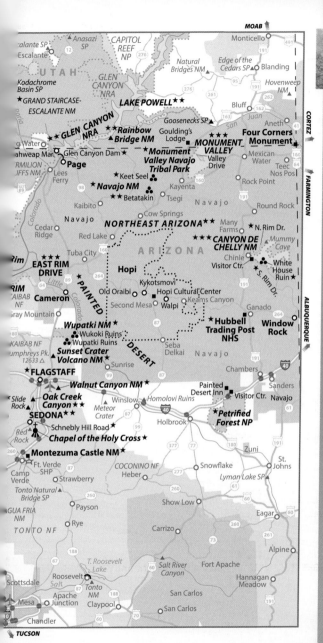

MOAB

Monticello

Escalante SP ▲ *Anasazi* CAPITOL
Escalante ▲ *SP* REEF
NP
UTAH 276

GLEN
Kodachrome CANYON
Basin SP NRA
★ GRAND STAIRCASE-
ESCALANTE NM
LAKE POWELL ★★

★★ GLEN CANYON NRA
Goosenecks SP ▲
Goulding's
Lodge
★★ *Rainbow*
▲ *Bridge NM* ★ Monument
Valley Navajo
Page ★ *Tribal Park*
★ Keet Seel

261
Natural
Bridges NM
Blanding
95
Edge of the
Cedars SP ▲
491
Hovenweep
NM ▲
191
Bluff 162
San Juan 163 Aneth
★★★ **Four Corners
Monument**
160 Mexican
Water 64
Teec
Nos Pos

g Water
ahweap Mar.
MILION
LIFFS NM
Glen Canyon Dam ★
Lees
Ferry

98 ★ *Navajo NM*
★★ *Betatakin*
Kayenta
Kaibito
Navajo
Cow Springs
Red Lake 160
NORTHEAST ARIZONA ★★
ARIZONA

Rock Point
191
Round Rock
Many
Farms N. Rim Dr.
★★★ **CANYON DE
CHELLY NM**
Mummy
Cave

Cedar
Ridge
Tuba City 160
Chinle
Visitor Ctr.
S. Rim Dr. ★
White
House
Ruin ★

Rim ★★★
EAST RIM
DRIVE
RIM 64
KAIBAB
NF
Gray Mountain
Cameron
PAINTED
Hopi
264 Old Oraibi
Kykotsmovi
Second Mesa Walpi
Hopi Cultural Center
Keams Canyon
191
Ganado
Hubbell
Trading Post
NHS

264
Window
Rock

ALBUQUERQUE

KAIBAB NF
umphreys Pk.
12633 △
Wupatki NM ★
Wukoki Ruins
Wupatki Ruins
Sunset Crater
Volcano NM ★
Sunrise
87
Seba
Delkai Navajo

FLAGSTAFF
Walnut Canyon NM ★
99
Chambers
191
40 Sanders
61

Slide ▲
Rock
Oak Creek
Canyon ★★
SEDONA ★★
Schnebly Hill Road ★
Chapel of the Holy Cross ★
Montezuma Castle NM ★
Winslow
Homolovi Ruins
Meteor
Crater
67
Holbrook

Painted
Desert Inn
Visitor Ctr.
Navajo
★ *Petrified
Forest NP*

Red
Rock
260
Ft. Verde
SHP
Camp
Verde 87 Strawberry
Tonto Natural
Bridge SP ▲
260 Payson
GUA FRIA
NM
TONTO NF
Rye
377 77
Zuni
Snowflake
Heber 227
Show Low
180
St.
Johns
Lyman Lake SP ▲
60
Eagar
261
Alpine

188
Roosevelt
Salt
T. Roosevelt
Lake
188
Tonto
NM
Claypool
Salt River
Canyon
73
Carrizo
Fort Apache
San Carlos
60 70
San Carlos
Hannagan
Meadow
191

Scottsdale
Mesa Apache
Junction
Chandler
60
TUCSON

GRAND CANYON

THE GREAT OUTDOORS

Canyon Floor Trails★

At Grand Canyon Village, the depth of the Grand Canyon—South Rim to canyon floor—is about 5,000ft. The distance on foot, via any of several steep and narrow trails, measures 7mi to 10mi. Most popular is the **Bright Angel Trail**, originating at Bright Angel Lodge in Grand Canyon Village. The trail descends 4,460ft in 9mi to the Colorado River to the **Phantom Ranch**, which lodges adventurers in cabins or dormitories. The trail is recommended only for exceptionally fit individuals. Hikers are strongly urged not to try hiking to the river and back to the rim in a single day. Adequate water, food and emergency supplies are essential, since midday heat during the summer months can pose extreme danger. It is also possible to ascend the other side of the canyon, arriving at the North Rim and to arrange transport back to the South Rim or your departure gateway.

Boat Beach, Phantom Ranch

NPS photo by Michael Quinn

Colorado River

Rafting the Colorado River is one of the best-known and most-sought river adventures in the US. Back in 1869, when Civil War veteran John Powell led an expedition down the canyon, he and his men were in small wooden boats. Today's inflatable pontoon rafts are much better suited for the churning river waters. Permits are limited so it's best to reserve far ahead. Several companies offer **guided rafting trips** in a range of distances and boat sizes, from one-day jaunts to week-long adventures. Advance bookings are essential—many trips are sold out a year ahead during popular times. For smooth-water trips *(1 day)*, contact **Colorado River Discovery** (888-522-6644; www.raftthecanyon.com). For multi-day whitewater rafting trips, visit www.nps.gov/grca.

🐴 Mule Trips

Daily departures year-round; $510 (fee includes overnight stay and meals at Phantom Ranch). Reservations required (book far in advance). 303-297-2757 or 888-297-2757. www.grandcanyon lodges.com.

A Grand Canyon tradition, rides on the back of a mule in a mule train have been popular here since the early 20C. This commercial option for descending to the canyon floor takes one day for the descent and one day for the return ascent, with lodging and meals provided at **Phantom Ranch** on the canyon floor. *This adventure is highly inappropriate for those with vertigo or any fear of heights.*

FOR KIDS

Junior Ranger Program

This National Park Service activity, available at all parks, is especially pertinent and popular at Grand Canyon because of the park's appeal to families. Unique programs include a special certification for kids who have made it, either on foot or mule, to the bottom of the canyon at Phantom Ranch.

As well, the park has various night programs for appreciating the star-lit canopy over the Grand Canyon. Check with the park visitor centers for times and locations of moon walks, graveyard walks and star talks. **The Twilight Zone** program is geared to families with children.

Celebrate Wildlife Day

NPS Photo by Erin Whittaker

A Sculpture Millions of Years Old

Billions of years ago the area now defined by the Grand Canyon was covered by shallow coastal waters and accented by active volcanoes. Over millions of years, layers of marine sediment and lava built to depths thousands of feet thick. About 1.8 billion years ago, heat and pressure from within the earth buckled the sedimentary layers into mountains 5-6mi high, changing their composition to a metamorphic rock called Vishnu schist. Molten intrusions in the mountains' core cooled and hardened into pink granite. Then erosion took over, reducing the mountains to mere vestiges over millions of years.

The process repeated itself: another shallow sea covering the land, more layers of sediment—12,000ft thick—were laid down. A new mountain range formed; erosion again assaulted the peaks so thoroughly that only ridges remained and, in many places, the ancient Vishnu schist was laid bare.

The horizontal layers above the schist, to 3,500ft below the modern canyon rim, were formed over 300 million years as oceans advanced across the Southwest, perhaps as many as seven times, and each time regressed. The environment was alternately marsh and desert, subject to rapid erosion. The era coincided with the age of dinosaurs and concluded about 65 million years ago with the end of the Cretaceous period. Then the Colorado River began to cut the canyon, gouging through rock and soil and carrying the debris away to sea. As erosion thinned the layer of rock above the earth's core, lava spewed to the surface. In fact, there have been several periods of recent volcanic activity in the Grand Canyon area, most recently in the 11C at Sunset Crater, southeast of the park near Flagstaff.

FOR KIDS

WESTERN GRAND CANYON

Contrary to popular perception, the Grand Canyon stretches far west beyond the main national park complex at South Rim, reaching almost 200mi downriver to Lake Mead National Recreation Area. The surrounding Colorado Plateau is a vast expanse of scrub pine, desert brush and sun-seared mesa, crossed by only a few gravel roads. In its far south portion is one of the longest remaining sections of historic **Route 66**, stretching 87mi between Seligman and Kingman. This is the province of raptors soaring high above, coyotes scrambling along gravel washes, ravens scratching the ground beside the road.

Two remote attractions, operated by Native American peoples who have inhabited this land for centuries, can be reached by a long journey from the main highway to the south edge of the canyon. The National Park controls the north side of the canyon in this remote stretch, but it is virtually all untracked wilderness.

Grand Canyon West and Skywalk★★

Hualapai Reservation. Accessible from I-40W and local roads; see website for directions. 928-769-2636 or 888-868-9378. www.grand canyonwest.com. Open Apr–Sept daily 7am–7pm. Rest of the year daily 8am–5pm. $82.

This tourism complex, a venture of the **Hualapai** tribe, is best-known for its **Skywalk★★**, a clear glass cantilevered "bridge" that extends 70ft out over the canyon below. Vertical drop directly beneath the walkway is about 800ft, the depth to the Colorado River surface nearly 4,000ft. The complex also includes **demonstration villages** of the region's Native American peoples, plus craft booths and food vendors. Most visitors arrive on tour buses from Las Vegas. Though private cars are welcome, portions of the access road are unpaved and may be difficult to travel in inclement weather. The Hualapai control a 108mi-long portion of the south rim, beginning about 50mi west of

Skywalk at Eagle Point

©Grand Canyon West

Grand Canyon Village.
The tribe has ambitious plans for a major travel resort centered on the Skywalk complex, with hotels, museums, restaurants, recreation facilities and even, some hope, a cable car extending to the canyon floor. Tribe members also operate **bus tours** and one- and two-day **rafting trips** on the Colorado River from Diamond Creek to Pearce Ferry. *A permit, available in Peach Springs or at the US 93 gateway south of Las Vegas, is required for private car travel off Route 66.*

Supai

Havasupai Reservation; foot and mule access only. From I-40W at Seligman, drive 34mi northwest on Rte. 66, then 65mi north on Tribal Road 18 to Hualapai Hilltop. Supai is another 10mi by trail. 928-448-2121; www.havasupaitribe.com.

The village of **Supai**, site of the Havasupai tribal center, lies at the bottom of Havasu Canyon, about 6mi from the Grand Canyon and the Colorado River. The Havasupai have lived here since at least the 16C. Several hundred tribal members continue to farm the fertile bottomlands, and in the recent past, provide tourism services.

Accessible only by foot, mule or helicopter, Supai has a small dormitory-style **tourist lodge** (*$; 24 rooms; 928-448-2111*), a restaurant, several shops, a campground and a post office. Visitors can see the farms and livestock areas kept along Havasu Creek by the Havasupai, and hike to the famous nearby turquoise-colored **waterfalls★★** pouring out of steep cliffs.

EXCURSIONS

⚜ Zion National Park★★★

From Grand Canyon's North Rim, drive north on Rte. 67 to US-89 A; continue north to Kanab, Utah; then take US-89, then Rte. 9 west, which accesses the park. Main visitor center open year-round daily 8am–5pm, extended evening hours in summer. 435-772-3256. www.nps.gov/zion. $25/vehicle (7-day pass).

Surrounding a 2,500ft-deep **sandstone canyon** decorated with waterfalls and damp, hanging gardens, Zion is one of the oldest (1919), best-known and most popular national parks. Its iconic and oft-photographed features include striated rock faces, towering sandstone monoliths and sparkling streams in shady canyons. More than 65mi of **hiking trails** lead into its backcountry wilderness. Non-hikers can go on horseback or join **shuttle-bus tours** *(Apr–Oct)* of the valley. Some 8mi long, .5mi wide and .5mi deep, Zion Canyon begins at the park's south entrance off Route 9. **Zion Scenic Canyon Drive** runs 8mi to the **Temple of Sinawava**, a natural sandstone amphitheater. *(Apr–Oct road is closed to private vehicles beyond historic Zion*

A Hardened Past

The massive sandstone features of Zion Canyon began forming 225 million years ago, when the area was an ancient sea floor. Later, it was a river delta and a lake bottom, and was covered in ash from volcanic eruptions. Shellfish flourished here; dinosaurs walked here. Around 170 million years ago, huge deposits of wind-blown sand left the region covered in dunes. Over time, the sand hardened into the 2,000ft-thick compacted sandstone that is now Zion's major geologic feature. Over the last 15 million years, a short span of geological time, the forces of the **Virgin River** began carving Zion Canyon. Even today, the river continues its carving: a million tons of rocky sediment are washed out of Zion Canyon yearly.

Lodge, 1mi from Route 9.) From the Temple, a paved 1mi trail follows the Virgin River to **The Narrows**, barely 20ft wide in the river bottom, squeezed between rock walls rising 2,000ft above it. Other sandstone monoliths include **The Watchman**, towering 2,555ft over the canyon floor; and the massive 7,810ft **West Temple**, standing more than 4,100ft above the river road. The **Great White Throne** is a prominent monolith that rises majestically 2,400ft behind a red-rock saddle. An attraction of a different sort, **Weeping Rock** is a cool rock niche carved over millennia by seeping water. Fertile hanging gardens thrive in the damp confines of its grotto. The **Kolob** area of Zion Park *(accessible only by road from I-15 Exit 40, 20mi south of Cedar City)* features a 5mi scenic drive along the Hurricane Fault, where twisted layers of exposed rock may be seen. Kolob's **Finger Canyons** extend southeast toward the main park area and are favored by backcountry hikers. A strenuous 7mi hike from Lee Pass, on La Verkin Creek, leads to **Kolob Arch**,

Great White Throne, Zion National Park

©National Park Service

one of the world's largest stone spans, at 310ft across.

A memorable drive into or out of the park, Route 9 east from Springdale to US-89, through 5,607ft-long **Zion Tunnel**, features six switchbacks; the tunnel was blasted out between 1927 and 1930. At the east end is **Checkerboard Mesa**, horizontal and vertical lines etched into the sandstone by geological fractures eroded by rain and snow.

🚶 Bryce Canyon National Park★★★

From Zion National Park, return to US-89 and head north 21mi to Rte. 12, then drive 13mi into the park. 435-834-5322. www.nps.gov/brca. $25/vehicle (7-day pass).

This 56sq mi park contains an array of rock spires, pinnacles, arches and hoodoos tinted in a palette of rich shades, considered by some to be the most brightly colored

rocks on earth. Red, yellow and brown shades derive from iron content; purple and lavender rocks contain more manganese. The odd rocks rise from the floor of a series of vast horseshoe-shaped natural amphitheaters. President Warren Harding declared the area a national monument in 1923; it became a national park in 1928.

An 18mi *(one-way)* **scenic drive** leads along the pine-clad rim top to popular views and trailheads leading down into the maze-like amphitheaters. Rim spots such as **Sunrise, Sunset, Rainbow** and **Inspiration Points**, all around 8,000ft elevation, afford differing views of the crenellated and sculpted rocks.

Hiking into Bryce Canyon provides a very different perspective of the rock forms. The park has more than 50mi of trails for hiking and horseback riding. Winter visitors, for whom the park may be virtually empty, cross-country ski on park

EXCURSIONS

Bryce Canyon National Park

©National Park Service

roads or borrow snowshoes (free) from the **Bryce Canyon Visitor Center** for ranger-guided tours.

🏞 Kodachrome Basin State Park★★

Off Rte. 12 from US-89. 435-679-8562. stateparks.utah.gov. $6.

The primary characteristic of this park is the concentration of numerous tall sandstone chimneys —sand pipes—that rise from the desert floor. The spires appear white or gray in midday light. In low-angle sun of early morning or late afternoon, they begin to glow in unexpected shades of crimson, mauve and burnished orange. The National Geographic Society explored and photographed the area for a story that appeared in the September 1949 issue of their magazine, using a new brand of Kodak film, from which the area gets its name.

Bryce's Background

The sculpted rocks began forming during the Cretaceous Period, around the time dinosaurs disappeared and flowering plants appeared. Deposits of sand and minerals, uplifts forced out of the earth, and erosional effects of rain and running water combined with snowfall, freezing and thawing to gradually remove billions of tons of rocks from the amphitheater rim. Eventually this debris was washed away by the **Paria River**, a tributary of the Colorado. Southern Paiute Indians lived around Bryce Canyon for hundreds of years prior to white settlement in the late 1800s. Native Americans called this place "red rocks standing like men in a bowl-shaped canyon." Americans shortened it to Bryce Canyon after rancher Ebenezer Bryce, who grazed livestock in the canyon bottoms in 1875 and called it "one hell of a place to lose a cow."

⚜ Grand Staircase-Escalante National Monument★

Access from Rte. 12. 435-826-5600 (Escalante visitor center) or 435-644-1300 (Kanab visitor center). www.ut.blm.gov/monument.

This national monument occupies 1.9 million acres of southern Utah wilderness west of the Waterpocket Fold and north of **Lake Powell★★**.

High, rugged and remote, the terrain rises 4,500ft above the Colorado River and Lake Powell, and is considered a geological sampler, containing a huge variety of sedimentary rock formations. It's been the subject of much political controversy over cattle grazing and proposals to drill for oil within the monument, which was established by executive order of President Bill Clinton in 1997. The **Grand Staircase**—mammoth cliffs and miles-long ledges formed into natural steps of colored rock strata—dominates its western third. Layer upon layer of rock composing the Pink, Gray, White, Vermilion and Chocolate Cliffs stretches across the horizon for a distance of more than 100mi.

The **Escalante River** flows from Boulder Mountain to Lake Powell in Glen Canyon National Recreation Area. The Escalante has carved deep canyons and gorges into an immense puzzle of sandstone mazes and slot canyons that offer extensive opportunities for self-sufficient and well-prepared backpackers and hikers. Services are available only in the adjacent communities of Boulder, Escalante, Cannonville and Kanab.

⚜ Cedar Breaks National Monument★★

Rte. 14 (23mi north of Rte. 9 via US-89 north) then Rte. 148. 435-586-0787. www.nps.gov/cebr. Facilities open late May–mid Oct daily. $4.

A 3mi-wide sandstone amphitheater is rimmed by millennia-old bristlecone pines, some of the oldest living plants on earth. Cedar Breaks' heavily eroded features are sculpted to a depth of 2,500ft below the 10,000ft rim in a series of rugged, narrow walls, fins, pinnacles, spires and arches. Mormon settlers misnamed the site for trees in the canyon bottom: they are junipers, not cedars. In winter Cedar Breaks road is impassable, but that makes it more appealing to cross-country skiers, who easily ascend the unplowed road from **Brian Head Resort** (*Rte. 143; 435-677-2035; www.brianhead.com*), just 3mi north. Brian Head is southern Utah's largest ski area; its base elevation of 9,600ft is the state's highest.

Touring Tip

Most Zion visitors approach the famous Mount Zion tunnel from the park's main Springdale entrance on the west side. The better approach is from the east (Rte. 9 from Mount Carmel Junction)—the direction you will be traveling if you come from Grand Canyon's North Rim. There's less traffic, and travelers are on the tunnel's north side and can better see the astounding views into Pine Creek Canyon from the tunnel's open galleries.

NORTHEAST ARIZONA★★

The northeast corner of Arizona—roughly 20,000 square miles lying north of Interstate 40 and east of Flagstaff, almost one-fifth of the state—was once popularly called "Indian Country." With good reason: here lie two Native American strongholds, the Navajo Nation and the Hopi enclave within it, that make this area the only major region in the Lower 48 states where indigenous peoples comprise the vast majority of the population—98 percent in the case of Navajo tribal lands.

It is also the home of some of the most iconic images of the **American West**—Monument Valley, the Painted Desert, Canyon de Chelly [pronounced Shay]. The arid landscape is riven by canyons, virtually bare of trees, seared by the sun and marked by towering mesas and monoliths that strive for the sky in majestic evidence of the millennial power of erosion. With little vegetative covering, the rock and sand shimmer in the sun in vibrant hues, while cottonball clouds ride summer thermals to the horizon. After dark, starlight paints the land or lightning storms rend the night from west to east in a show visible for miles.

The landscape has made an indelible impression on the human imagination from its starring role in dozens of classic **Western movies**, most famously the John Ford/John Wayne titles such as *Stagecoach* and *My Darling Clementin*. The latter a retelling of the story of Wyatt Earp and the OK Corral gunfight, which actually took place 300 miles south at Tombstone rather than the distinctive **Monument Valley** landscape in which most filming was done. This region today draws travelers intent on experiencing **Native culture**, marveling at the superlative landscape and treading in the footsteps of history.

It's an area unique in North America, a place where the Navajo use of the term "nation" is far more than superficial. Both **Hopi** and **Navajo** believe this earth represents the "fourth world" of human existence; to the Navajo, the "Glittering World."

Hubbell Trading Post National Historic Site

©Leslie Forsberg/Michelin

Practical Information

Getting There and Getting Around

♦ **By Air** – The main gateways to Northeast Arizona are Flagstaff (FLG) and Albuquerque (ABQ); each has an airport, though Flagstaff's has limited service consisting of several flights a day from Phoenix. Las Vegas (LAS) and Phoenix (PHX) provide air connections throughout North America, Europe and Asia. Flagstaff is 250 miles (4 hours) from Las Vegas, and 156 miles (2.5 hours) from Phoenix. Window Rock, capital of the Navajo Nation, is 170 miles (2.5 hours) from Albuquerque.

♦ **By Train** – Amtrak serves Flagstaff twice daily on the Southwest Chief line; it also stops in Gallup, New Mexico; www.amtrak.com.

♦ **By Car** – Interstate 40 is the main thoroughfare through Northern Arizona, connecting the region to Los Angeles (467mi, 7.5hrs) and Albuquerque (328mi, 5hrs). Interstate 17 connects Flagstaff to Phoenix, a 156mi drive of 2.5hrs. US Hwys 89, 160 and 191 are the main arteries through Navajoland; all are high-speed roads maintained in winter.

Many secondary roads in Northeast Arizona are gravel and, while quite passable in good weather, may be treacherous in the winter and during rainstorms. Established roads within the Navajo Nation are open to the public, but most unpaved or un-numbered roads are private. Navajoland is also subject to summertime thunderstorms that produce **flash flooding**, and it is imperative that drivers not take their cars into lowlying washes, gullies and underpasses during heavy rains. Caution signs identify washes subject to flooding, and it's important to note that a lowlying area may carry floodwaters born in mountains far away and can flood even though skies are clear directly overhead.

Visitor Information

Tourists are welcome on the reservations; checking the tribe's website in advance of your visit is highly recommended.
Useful websites are www.discovernavajo.com; general information, www.navajo-nsn.gov; www.hopi-nsn.gov.

Reservation Time

The Navajo Nation observes **Daylight Saving Time**, while the state of Arizona and Hopi reservation do not. Therefore, from March through October, the reservation is an hour ahead of Arizona (and Hopi) and on the same time as New Mexico, while Arizona (and Hopi) are an hour behind and on the same time as California. For example, there is an hour difference between the time in Window Rock and Flagstaff. From early November to early March, Arizona, Hopi and the Navajo Nation are all on the same time.

Removal is Illegal

Please note that removal of any natural or historic item is illegal within any of the many parks and preserves in this region. Pottery shards, arrowheads, rock specimens, bird feathers and the like all are protected by federal law.

NORTHEAST ARIZONA

NAVAJO NATION

Alcohol is prohibited within Navajo Nation boundaries.

Comprising most of the northeast corner of Arizona, plus adjacent portions of Utah and New Mexico, the centuries-old home of the Navajo people is the largest **Indian reservation** in the US. The tribal capital is **Window Rock**, 188mi (3hrs) northeast of Flagstaff via Interstate 40 and Highway 12. It is a self-governing sovereign entity within the US—Diné Bikéyah (land of the people) in the Navajo tongue. Though the land they inhabit is the epitome of arid desert country, the people of Navajoland actually have their origins in the northlands of Canada; they and the Apaches are linguistically **Athabascan** and thus related to the indigenous peoples of the Alaskan and Yukon interior. Anthropologists believe the Navajo and Apache began to move south into their current home around 1300 AD, and the former had established their present-day nation by 1700, subsisting on dryland agriculture, hunting and trading; and by herding a hardy breed of sheep, the Churro, that they'd obtained from Spanish friars in the 16C.

Navajoland was Mexican territory until 1848; prior to US annexation, Navajo and Apache bands were in a state of frequent war with Spanish and Mexican authorities and other Southwest native peoples. American troops forced Navajos to relocate to Fort Sumner, New Mexico in 1846, during the notorious **Long Walk** during which the people endured many privations; hundreds died. The Navajo returned to their homeland after the **Treaty of 1848**, which established what was then a relatively small reservation shortly at the same time the entire area was formally added to the US. Expanded considerably since then, the reservation was first governed by a formal tribal council in 1923. In 1989 the tribe adopted a **constitutional democracy** under which the nation is governed by an elected president, the **Navajo Nation Council**, and an independent judiciary. The Navajos operate their own parks, school system, college, environmental protection, economic development and natural resources departments; and most famously, their own police, immortalized by New Mexico author **Tony Hillerman** in a much-beloved series of mysteries set on the reservation, including

---

Fast Facts

Land area: 27,000 square miles in Arizona, Utah and New Mexico; roughly equal to West Virginia.

Population: 201,000 enrolled tribal members within the reservation boundaries; 300,000 total.

Highest point: Navajo Mountain, northern Arizona, 10,388 feet

Average annual precipitation: 6 to 20 inches

Temperature range: near zero in winter to 110°F in summer

What's in a Name?

Not one but two commonly used names for Southwest peoples are, in fact, derived from "foreign" tongues and reflect cultural misplacements that have become English-language mainstays by default. The first is the name for the USA's largest Indian reservation: the **Diné** are widely known as the Navajo—even by themselves, although a proposal to revive the name Diné was formally rejected by the Navajo Nation Council in 1994. The word "Navajo" is actually a modification of the Spanish term *"Apaches del Nabaju,"* which means "Apaches who farm in the valley"—*nabaju* being the Spanish corruption of the Tew'a Pueblo term for farm fields in a valley, and **Apache** representing the close cultural relationship of the Apache and Navajo peoples (both are Athabascan in origin). Despite its unofficial status, the term Diné sees many uses within Navajoland.

Meanwhile, the ancestors of the Pueblo peoples now found throughout the Southwest were long called the **Anasazi**, and during most of the 20C were considered a "lost" people who had vanished from the earth after abandoning communities such as Mesa Verde and Chaco Canyon. But anthropologists now know they simply became, or joined, today's Pueblo peoples—Taos, Acoma and more. Archaeologists and other scientists today use the term **Ancestral Puebloans** instead of "Anasazi"—which is a Navajo (Diné) word that means "enemy ancestors." Within Navajoland, the terms tribe, nation and reservation are all in common use, though "nation" is the formal designation. The same is true for *Native American* and *Indian*—just as *US citizen* and *American* have nearly identical meanings. Most Native Americans would prefer to be known by their individual affiliations, such as Navajo, Diné or **Hopi**.

such titles as *The Blessing Way, A Thief of Time* and *Listening Woman*. Hillerman's books brought such attention to Navajoland that his daughter, Anne Hillerman, wrote a travel guide to the area, *Tony Hillerman's Landscape: On the Road with Chee and Leaphorn*, a reference to her father's two tribal police characters, Jim Chee and Joe Leaphorn.

While the tribe has embraced modern life, that includes some of the problems common to many 21C societies, such as high unemployment and substance abuse. As many as 50 percent of Navajoland tribal members lack jobs—though many pursue livelihoods devoted to arts, crafts and food preparation. Navajo traditions such as the **hogan** endure: the round or six-sided house may now be made of concrete block rather than adobe or small timber, but the door will still face east to welcome the rising sun. Many Navajo households today have both modern houses and a hogan, and such homesteads are common sights as visitors travel throughout Navajoland. So are the fine **rugs**, both decorative and functional, that have been woven by Navajo people for centuries.

Modern travelers can find both present-day and traditional

Window Rock

©beejal mehta/iStockphoto.com

versions of these. The latter are made of wool carded and spun by hand, using only natural dyes, and are beautiful works of art well worth the hundreds or sometimes thousands of dollars they cost; they are accurate reflections of the spiritual depth of life practiced by the artisans of this unique place. While seeing these vast tribal lands requires a lot of traveling, it's worth it to heed a common Navajo proverb and observe the special place you are visiting: "Be still, and the earth will speak to you."

The drive in Navajo Tribal Park's portion of Monument Valley is open to visitors (fee applies), but is not recommended for passenger cars. The tribe offers 4WD and horseback tours, with expert narration.

An Unbreakable Code

American forces fighting the Japanese in World War II early on faced a difficult problem: they could not create a code that Japanese cryptographers were unable to break. "Surprise" attacks and US troop movements were thus exposed—until a soldier whose father had been a missionary in Navajoland had a startling idea: enlist Navajo speakers to transmit messages. The language had no alphabet, was very difficult to learn, was virtually unknown outside the US, and could be adapted easily for military use. Eventually more than 400 **code talkers** served as US Marines in the Pacific War, and their efforts were key to the war effort. Most notably, during the American assault on Iwo Jima, more than 800 coded messages were a crucial part of the eventual US victory.

After the war, the US government classified the story of the code talkers, and their heroism was not publicly revealed until 1968. Today, a small exhibit in **Kayenta** documents this amazing story *(in the Burger King shopping center on Hwy. 160)*, and a similar exhibit occupies a small annex in the **Tuba City Trading Post** *(10 N. Main St.)*. Efforts are underway to raise money for a memorial complex that will be the **National Navajo Code Talkers Museum and Veterans Center** in Window Rock, the Navajo capital. For more information visit www.navajocodetalkers.org.

HISTORICAL SITES

Monument Valley ★★★

Straddling the Utah-Arizona border along US-163, north of Kayenta.

This famous landscape, whose towering buttes form majestic monuments against the surrounding desert plains, is well-known to Western movie fans around the world. A good impression of the area can be obtained simply by driving the stretch of US 163 between Kayenta, Arizona, and Bluff, Utah. The approach from the north affords a splendid **panorama★★** in late afternoon when the buttes are backlit by the westering sun. The most authentic experience of the landscape can be found at **Monument Valley Navajo Tribal Park★** *(entrance on US-163, just north of the Utah/Arizona state line; open May–Sept daily 6am–8pm; til 5pm rest of the year; $5; 435-727-5874; navajonationparks.org; high-clearance vehicles advised),* a preserve southeast of US-163 through which an unpaved 17mi *(40 min)* **scenic road** winds.

The tribal park holds the most compelling sections of what the Navajo call "Valley of the Rocks." Drivers on the road pass formations with names such as Mitten Buttes, Rain God Mesa, Spearhead Mesa, Totem Pole and the Thumb. The new (2008) Navajo-owned **View Hotel** is a red-toned, 95-room facility set in a saddle with a splendid view of the valley and easy access to the one **hiking trail** visitors can walk without a guide. A campground, picnic facilities and small visitor center also greet visitors. On the other side of the highway, at the conspicuous **Goulding's Lodge** *(Goulding's Rd., 435-727-3231; www.gouldings.com),* a small **museum** recounts the history of the famous movies filmed here.

Hubbell Trading Post National Historic Site★

US-264, 1mi west of Ganado. Tours of the Hubbell home $2. Open Oct–mid-May daily 8am–5pm; til 6pm summer. 928-755-3475. www.nps.gov/hutr.

Monument Valley

HISTORICAL SITES

These sturdy, low-slung **adobe buildings** occupy a serene spot beneath cottonwood trees along Pueblo Colorado Wash. Travelers, traders and Navajos have been visiting this place since 1878; it played a key role in helping the Navajo reestablish their lives in Arizona when they returned from their forced incarceration in New Mexico. The 160-acre site sits at 6,300 ft about halfway between Window Rock and Canyon de Chelly.

The trading post still operates today, staffed by a nonprofit association since the Hubbell family sold the property to the National Park Service in 1968. Most of its goods now consist of handsome **Navajo rugs**, baskets, pottery and other crafts, as well as a smattering of groceries. The site's **interpretive center** is staffed by Navajo and Hopi interpreters, who explain traditional lifestyles in Navajoland and offer expert advice to visitors.

MONUMENTS

Canyon de Chelly National Monument★★★

Chinle, Arizona. Visitor center 2mi east of US-191 along Tribal Rte. 7; open year-round daily 8am–5pm. Canyon scenic drive roads open year-round, though they may be closed during inclement weather. 928-674-5500. www.nps.gov/cach.

The National Park Service and Navajo Nation jointly manage the park; admission for the scenic drives is free. Two paved scenic roads traverse the **South Rim★** of Canyon de Chelly and the **North Rim★** of adjacent Canyon del Muerto. Overlooks and viewpoints with parking are numerous, each providing a unique vantage into the canyon depths. Especially rewarding overlooks on the south side are White House, Sliding House and Spider Rock. On the north side, overlooks permit views of Antelope House and Massacre

Canyon de Chelly National Monument

©Leslie Forsberg/Michelin

Cave, where Spanish soldiers slaughtered 115 Navajos in 1805. Except for one trail *(see below)*, entry into the canyon is restricted to those traveling with authorized Navajo guides. **Tours** are given in specially equipped vehicles, on horseback, or on foot *(rates vary from $50 up)*. Reservations for tours are advised in the busy summer season for those traveling from afar who have only one or two days at the park.

Visitors not taking an authorized tour may enter the canyon by way of the **White House Trail★**, a steep descent *(1mi round-trip; allow 2hrs, bring water and sun protection)* into the canyon floor leading to the **White House Ruin★**, a multistory cliff dwelling. Though arduous, the hike is a rewarding trip into a separate world.

Navajo National Monument★

10mi north of US-60, at the end of Rte 564. Visitor center open late May–early Sept daily 8am–5:30pm; rest of the year daily 9am–5pm. Note that the monument observes Daylight Saving Time, and that flash flooding periodically closes the canyon. 928-672-2700. www.nps.gov/nava.

Sequestered here in remote Tsegi Canyon in far northern Arizona is a collection of Ancestral Puebloan cliff dwellings similar to the larger and better-known ones at Mesa Verde. Built of adobe and stone, they date from 1250 AD or so, and are in relatively good condition. Visitors can admire the roof beams, masonry work, rock art and other features typical of the era. Three short **self-guided**

trails lead visitors along the cliff edge opposite for views of the ruins from afar. **Ranger-guided hikes** to the ruins depart from the visitor center daily in summer. Tours to the impressive 135-room **Betatakin ruins★★** depart daily *(8:15am and 10am)*; both are strenuous treks of 3mi or 5mi with substantial elevation changes. Occasional hikes might be available in winter *(call ahead to check)*.

The daily hike to the larger, 160-room **Keet Seel★** site is a rigorous 17mi round-trip trek, and requires advance reservations, with a backcountry permit; visitors may elect to stay overnight here.

Four Corners Monument Tribal Park

Just off US-160, 6mi north of Teec Nos Pos. Open year-round daily 8am–7pm (til 5pm in winter). navajonationparks.org. $3.

This location is the only point in the USA where four states meet—a cartographical happenstance—but nonetheless the object of much fascination by over-the-road travelers. A granite and brass **marker** indicates the precise spot of the four corners. Lines designate each state boundary, and visitors delight in standing in two, three or all four states all at once, cameras clicking. Navajo artisans and food vendors operate numerous stands surrounding the park. *Note that Navajo belief considers cremation unacceptable, and it is thus a violation of Navajo culture and sovereignty to bring remains to Four Corners, or any other Navajo Nation land, to fling them in the wind.*

THE GREAT OUTDOORS

🦌 Navajo Nation Zoo and Botanical Park★

34 Rte. 264, Window Rock. Open Mon–Sat 10am–4:30pm. 928-871-6574. www.navajozoo.org.

This Navajo-owned, free-admission facility operated in Window Rock offers visitors an opportunity to view the native animals and plants of Navajoland, from coyotes to cougars, and rabbitbrush to ponderosa pine. Picnic facilities and environmental education exhibits enhance the experience. Nearby, **Window Rock** is a small arch in a sandstone ridge from which the Navajo capital takes its name; the tribal offices are close by. A small memorial near the base of the arch honors Navajo soldiers who have served in the US armed forces, including the famous "Code Talkers" (navajonationparks.org)

Painted Desert★

From Petrified Forest northwest to Tuba City; best viewed along US-89 north of Flagstaff.

Beautiful striations of pastel colors truly do "paint" the salt-pans,

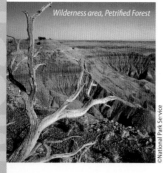
Wilderness area, Petrified Forest
©National Park Service

cliffs and buttes in this region of Navajoland that bestrides the southwest corner of the Navajo Nation. Ranging from crimson, fuchsia and lavender to ochre and chartreuse, the clays, sands and sandstones of the region are memorably colored, and often lie exposed in layered formations. Most of the Painted Desert lies far off-road and is accessible only to guided treks, but innumerable highway-side overlooks offer good views of this famous landscape.

Petrified Forest★

I-40, Exit 311, 26mi east of Holbrook. 928-524-6228. www.nps.gov/pefo.

An immense and colorful concentration of petrified wood and fossils, more than 225 million years old, spreads out over the striated, pastel-hued badlands of the Painted Desert. The main park road runs 28mi between I-40 and US-180, an easy detour from the interstate. At its north end, the **Painted Desert Visitor Center** offers a 20min film and exhibits. Two miles up the road is the **Painted Desert Inn** (1924), a National Historical Landmark. The structure was originally a trading post, then an inn; it's now a museum and gift shop. **Overlooks** on the southbound road pass 13C Ancestral Puebloan ruins and a landscape strewn with colorful petrified logs. Several short hikes access off-road areas.

Removal of rock specimens is illegal, though an estimated 12 tons of the fossil wood is stolen from the Petrified Forest each year.

HOPI RESERVATION

Rte. 264 between Tuba City and Granado. wwwvisithopi.com.

Occupying an "island" completely surrounded by the Navajo Nation, the Hopi Reservation—also known as just Hopi—encompasses 2,531 sq mi about 70mi northeast of Flagstaff. Here, 7,000 Hopi and Tewa people live in a dozen villages near and on three mesas (First, Second and Third), which tribal tradition says have been their home for more than 100 generations. The Hopi are a Puebloan people, related to the tribes that dwell in similar pueblos in New Mexico. They have zealously guarded their traditional lifestyles in modern times, reserving special status for corn and **Maasaw**, the caretaker of the earth. Theirs is the only Puebloan enclave in Arizona. The Hopi people endeavor to live as peaceful, respectful farmers. Though the Hopi treasure their role as perhaps the most traditional of all American tribes, visitors are welcome on Hopi lands; many come to observe **special dances** and ceremonies. Some, though not all, of these are open to the public. For all such occasions, the Hopi *forbid photography, videography, sketching and audio recording. Visitors are also asked to honor the privacy of the dwellings within the villages; for more information consult www.visithopi.com.*

Several villages have **artisan galleries** offering katsina (kachina) dolls, pottery and other traditional arts. Two inns provide accommodations and dining within the reservation: the **Hopi Cultural Center★** Restaurant & Inn at Second Mesa *(www.hopiculturalcenter. com)*; and the **Moenkopi Legacy Inn & Suites** at Kayenta, just outside Tuba City *(1 Legacy Lane; experiencehopi.com)*. Both facilities also contain art and craft galleries that are excellent places to obtain authentic Hopi goods.

Dances Divine

Vivid costumes, elaborate scores and choreography make the many Hopi ceremonial dances among the best-known aboriginal arts in North America. The dances honor and reflect the natural forces the Hopi regard as sacred, such as rain, corn, animals and natural spirits. At the same time, they accomplish important cultural functions and values reinforcement. For instance, the late summer **Butterfly Dance**, an intricate two-day event whose participants must memorize 32 songs and chants, is meant to help pair young men and women. The **Snake Dance** calls for rain; the **Bean Dance** is a planting time ceremony. Visitors to Hopi villages are welcome to watch dances open to the public—but not private ceremonies and dances. Schedules may be found online at several visitor sites, such as experiencehopi.com. In the villages, signs indicate a ceremony's public or private status. *Even at public dances, no recording of any sort—photography, videography or sound recording, not even sketching—is permitted.* The prohibition dates to an episode in which sacred Hopi dances were inappropriately depicted in a mass-market comic book. Visitors are asked to watch quietly only.

EXCURSIONS

🚳 Mesa Verde National Park★★★

From Four Corners Monument, drive 39mi northeast to Cortez, Colorado, via US-160. National park gateway lies10mi east of Cortez, off US-160. $15 (free Jan–Feb). Open daily year-round; numerous seasonal variations among park centers and facilities, include the best-known cliff-houses. Roads, trails and access to the ruins may be closed due to weather. 970-529-4465. www.nps.gov/meve.

The most impressive remnants of an abandoned pre-Columbian civilization in the US occupy sheltered cliff ledges within a vast mesa rising above the desert plains of southwest Colorado. Here are more than 600 cliff dwellings and 5,000 known archaeological sites, most tucked within deep canyons that drop south toward New Mexico's San Juan River basin. A **World Heritage Site** (1978), this famous park preserves both an outstanding natural landscape and the evidence of a people who flourished here from AD 500 to 1300.

A long drive from the valley floor north of the mesa carves its way up to the park's **Far View Visitor Center★★** sitting at 8,500ft. Here travelers learn the once-mysterious story of the **Ancestral Puebloan** peoples who lived in the cliff dwellings scattered among the canyons. Long thought to have "disappeared," they are now known to have simply abandoned this area and formed, or assimilated, into the many pueblos southward in New Mexico.

While here, they built complex villages beneath overhanging cliffs, hunted in the canyon bottoms and grew corn, beans, squash and other foods on the mesa top above. The best-known dwellings such as **Cliff Palace★★★, Spruce Tree House★★★, Long House★★** and **Balcony House★★** are all large (up to 150 rooms), impressive examples of their builders' masonry skill. Most must be visited by **ranger-led tour**, and

Mesa Verde National Park

©National Park Service

can involve steep climbs on access ladders. The echoes of ancient North American history whisper in each of the ruins: a visit prompts thoughtful travelers to mull the ebb and flow of human affairs. Lodging inside the park is provided by Aramark Corp. at the distinctive, native-stone **Far View Lodge** near the visitor center *(800-449-2288 or 602-331-5210; www.vistimesaverde.com)*. Southwest-style furnishings enhance the lodge's ambience, and all the rooms enjoy expansive views

🛶 Glen Canyon National Recreation Area★★

From US-160 south of Navajo NM, take Rte. 98 northwest 66mi to Page, Arizona, then US-89. 928-608-6200. www.nps.gov/glca.

This vast area extends from Canyonlands National Park southwest to Grand Canyon National Park, covering more than 1,900sq mi. **Lake Powell★★**, its centerpiece, is a huge recreational playground, whose watery fingers reach into sandy coves, inlets and slot canyons, between towering red-rock cliffs to depths of 500ft. The waters, which took 17 years to fill to a surface elevation of 3,700ft above sea level, provide opportunities for houseboating, power boating, fishing and water skiing. On the lake are four **marinas** and several **campgrounds**.

In the surrounding lands, with their myriad inlets and coves, side canyons protect ancient ruins and natural stone features, including arches and bridges, pinnacles, fins, towers and stone chimneys known as **sand pipes**. Backcountry **trails** are extensive throughout.

🛶 Glen Canyon Dam★

US-89, 2mi northwest of Page. 928-608-6404. www.nps.gov/glca.

The dam produces more than 1300 megawatts of electricity, serving Utah, Colorado, Wyoming, Arizona and New Mexico. With all eight of its generators operating, 15 million gallons of water pass through the dam each minute. The **Carl B. Hayden Visitors Center** *(US-89; 928-608-6404)* provides an overview of operations, and **guided tours** of the dam *($5)*.

🛶 Rainbow Bridge National Monument★★

520-608-6200. www.nps.gov/rabr.

One of the most impressive stone formations in the Southwest, Rainbow Bridge stands 290ft above the shores of Lake Powell, beside an inlet just inside the Utah border with Arizona. Higher than the US Capitol Building in Washington, DC, it spans 275ft, nearly the length of a football field. It's called *Nonnezoshi* ("rainbow turned to stone") by the Navajo, who believe that passing beneath Rainbow Bridge without offering special prayers will bring misfortune. The bridge has long been sacred to both the Navajo and the Paiute people of the interior Southwest. *To respect these beliefs, the Park Service asks visitors to refrain from walking under the bridge.*

Boat tours depart daily from **Wahweap Marina**, north of the Glen Canyon Dam, and cover the 50mi to Rainbow Bridge.

EXCURSIONS

WEST ARIZONA

West of Flagstaff, off I-40, a remnant of historic Route 66 stretches from Ash Fork west to Kingman. Along the state's western border, the Colorado River flows southward through Lake Mead, a vast recreational lake formed by one of the world's best-known (and earliest) major hydroelectric projects, Hoover Dam. Not far across the border, in Nevada, Las Vegas remains the undisputed global playground for adults seeking high-stakes gambling, high-octane entertainment and high-voltage buzz. Back in Arizona, the Colorado River courses southward through Lake Havasu, site of the famed London Bridge, and along the Bill Williams River National Wildlife Refuge. Inland to the east, another river, the Hassayampa, heads toward the charming town of Wickenburg, once the "dude" ranch capital of the state.

CITIES

Kingman★

I-40, Rtes. 66 and 93. Visitor center at 120 Andy Devine Ave; 928-753-6106 or 866-427-7866; www.gokingman.com.

This crossroads town prospered as a railway hub at the turn of the 19C and in the 1930s as a stop-over for travelers along Route 66. The train still stops here—Amtrak's Chicago-Los Angeles line—and, though Route 66 was replaced by I-40, the last and longest stretch of the historic road nearby draws history buffs and classic-car enthusiasts. Kingman's **downtown** holds nearly two-dozen historic sites

and structures dating from the highway's heyday or before. Among them, along **Andy Devine Avenue** (yes, the character actor in many Western films was raised here), is Kingman's **Powerhouse Visitor Center** (1907) with the **Route 66 Museum** inside it (*see Museums*). Both the **Mohave County Courthouse** (*4th and Oak Sts.*) and **Bonelli House★** (*430 E. Spring St.; 928-753-3195; guided tours Mon–Fri, $2*) were built in 1915 of tufa stone. For a return to the 1950s, have lunch at **Mr. D'z Route 66 Diner**, complete with jukebox and turquoise vinyl banquettes (*105 E. Andy Devine Ave.; 928-718-0066; www.mrdzroute66diner.com*). West of Kingman, **Lake Mead National Recreation Area★** embraces North America's largest reservoir. **Lake Mead** has brought boating, fishing, water skiing and other water sports to an arid land.

Wickenburg★

Rtes. 60 and 93. Visitor center in historic train depot, 216 N. Frontier St.; 928-684-5479; www. outwickenburgway.com; map and walking-tour brochure available.

Sign above Mr. D'z Route 66 Diner

©Gwen Cannon/Michelin

Get Your Kicks on the Mother Road

Long before most Americans ever considered cross-country travel, a new ribbon of asphalt changed the country's perception of itself. In 1928 **Route 66** creased the continental US like a bowline—one of the first national highways, and a migration route for families fleeing the 1930s Dust Bowl for California. From 1945 to 1955, car ownership doubled nationally, sparking a country-wide penchant for "road trips." The 1950s song "Get your kicks on Route 66" and a 1960s television series sealed the fame of the "Mother Road."

In actuality, the highway covers just two-thirds of the US, 2,400mi from Chicago to Los Angeles; its best-known stretch lies between Albuquerque and California's Mojave Desert, along which motels, small diners and other tourist sites sprang up to serve travelers. Replaced by modern four-lane interstates such as I-40, the highway was officially decommissioned in 1985. It immediately gained cult status. For more information, access the National Park Service guide at www.nps.gov/nr/travel/route66.

This delightful town retains its Wild West flavor in more than 25 historic buildings, including its **train depot** (1895) and 1905 **schoolhouse**, as well as modern-day shops and restaurants selling Western wares and grub. Sited near the Hassayampa River, the former mining and ranching town was named for businessman Henry Wickenburg, from whose now-defunct **Vulture Mine** gold worth millions of dollars was extracted

(*2hr tours Sat 10am; $10; www.vultureminetours.com*). In the 1930s and 40s, several area cattle ranches hosted overnight guests, offering them an "Out West" experience of trail rides and campfire cookouts, in addition to the salubrious desert climate. Rancho de los Caballeros, Flying E Ranch and a few other area ranches continue to welcome overnight guests (*see Hotels*). You'll also be welcome at **Nana's Sandwich Saloon** downtown (*48*

©Gwen Cannon/Michelin

Little Red Schoolhouse, Wickenburg

The Bolo

Arizona's bolo ties—those thin, ropelike necklaces looped through a (usually turquoise) pendant—are a key accessory of Western garb. Wickenburg native Vic Cedarstaff claims to have invented them in 1949. A fine bolo collection can been seen in the Desert Caballeros Western Museum, including Cedarstaff's original design.

N. Tegner St.; 928-684-5539), where locals gather for coffee inside or on the pleasant patio out back.

Lake Havasu City

Rte. 95, 19mi south of I-40.
Visitor center at 422 English Village
(near the bridge). 928-855-5655.
www.golakehavasu.com.

Known for its famed 1,000ft-long **London Bridge**, this city of 53,000 residents overlooks the namesake lake that beckons water enthusiasts of every stripe. **Parker Dam** was completed in 1938, creating a reservoir in the Colorado River with a 450mi shoreline. Originally over the River Thames in London, England, the then sinking bridge was purchased for $2,460,000 by Lake Havasu City's founder, and opened here in 1971 after reassembly (total cost was $7.5 million); it spans a mile-long channel of water flowing in from Lake Havasu. For boat rentals, fishing charters and lake tours, visit the city's website (*see above*).

Touring Tip

For a short voyage, take Havasu Landing Resort Casino's ferry (*30min each way; $2 round-trip*) from English Village (*schedules available at the visitor center*) across Lake Havasu to the California side. Simply disembark at the casino dock, then reboard in 5min for the return passage.

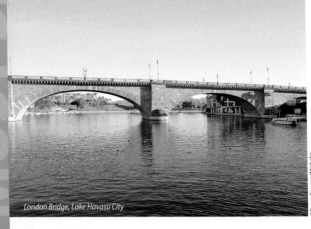

London Bridge, Lake Havasu City

©Gwen Cannon/Michelin

MUSEUMS

Desert Caballeros Western Museum★★★

21 N. Frontier St., Wickenburg. 928-684-2272. www.western museum.org. Open year-round Mon–Sat 10am–5pm, Sun noon–4pm. Closed major holidays and Mon late May–early Sept. $7.50.

This compact, two-level museum in Wickenburg's historic core houses an extraordinarily rich collection of Western Americana, ranging from oils by the grand masters of Western art to cowboy accoutrements. The highlight is the remarkable **Hays' Spirit of the Cowboy Collection★★★** of chaps, hats, spurs, bandanas, guns, lariats and other cowboy paraphernalia well displayed as singular categories. Paintings and sculpture on Western topics include exquisite works by Frederic Remington, Charles Russell, George Catlin, Thomas Moran and other artists. Downstairs, re-created settings such as the interior of a general store evoke life at the turn of the 19C. Two **museum shops** stock an array of quality gift items, including Western wares and home decor.

Mohave Museum of History and Arts★★

400 W. Beale St., Kingman. 928-753-3195. www.mohavemuseum. org. Open year-round Mon–Fri 9am–5pm, Sat 1pm–5pm. Closed major holidays. $4 (ticket also valid for Bonelli House and Route 66 Museum).

This nondescript warehouse-size building holds within an astonishing quantity of artifacts and memorabilia that trace the region's past. A re-created **wikieup** introduces the Native American galleries, whose highlights are splendid collections of Navajo rugs, baskets and kachina (or katsina) dolls. Exhibits devoted to mining, train travel and ranching are also of special interest.

Route 66 Museum★

In Powerhouse Visitor Center, 120 Andy Devine Ave., Kingman. 928-753-9889. www.route66museum. net. Open year-round daily 9am–5pm. $4 (ticket valid for Bonelli House and Mohave Museum).

This extensive museum presents a most informative walk-through time line of periods in the history of the **Mother Road**. Exhibits include photographs, maps, artifacts, furnishings, mannequins in period dress, old gas pumps and a vintage Studebaker.

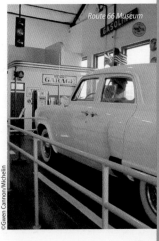

Route 66 Museum

©Gwen Cannon/Michelin

THE GREAT OUTDOORS

Bill Williams River National Wildlife Refuge★

60911 Hwy. 95 in Parker, 18mi south of Lake Havasu City. 928-667-4144. www.fws.gov. Visitor center open year-round Mon–Fri 8am–4pm; closed major holidays; map and literature available.

This 6,000-acre riparian reserve along the Colorado River has been a refuge since 1941. It's named for **William Sherley Williams** (1787-1849), a skilled trapper, Indian-language interpreter and guide from North Carolina who traveled widely in the West.

Wading birds, such as **snowy egrets**, as well as ducks like grebes and mallards, flock to the watery oasis. On the peninsula and mainland **trails**, visitors will undoubtedly see many of the birds of the 350 species found here.

Bill Williams River National Wildlife Refuge

©Gwen Cannon/Michelin

Joshua Forest Parkway★

Rte. 93 between I-40 (18mi east of Kingman) and Wickenburg.

A memorable drive, this 91mi stretch of paved road (Route 93) leads through desert scrublands, parallels the Big Sandy River near the hamlet of **Wikieup** (the official start of the scenic byway) and climbs up the Aquarius Mountains—whose peaks hover between 6,000 and 7,000ft—before entering an outcropping of boulders and cutting through a forest of hundreds of **joshua trees**. The signature plant of the Mojave Desert, they are neither trees nor cactus, but large **yuccas** that can reach above 40ft and live for hundreds of years. The trunks are composed of densely packed layers of fiber, not wood.

Hassayampa River Preserve

49614 N. US-60, about 3mi southeast of Wickenburg. 928-684-2772. nature.org/hassayampa. Open mid-May–mid Sept Wed–Sun 8am–5pm. Rest of the year Fri–Sun 7am–11am. Closed major holidays. $5 donation (members $3). Trail map available at visitor center.

A **loop trail** in The Nature Conservancy's 700-acre preserve encircles spring-fed **Palm Lake**, and winds amid Royal palm, cottonwood and willow trees; other trails parallel a stretch of the 100mi-long river, which flows mostly underground. Get a bird checklist from the visitor center for this important birding site.

WEST ARIZONA

MUST DO

EXCURSIONS

🏛 Hoover Dam★★★

US-93, 73mi northwest of Kingman. 702-494-2517. www.usbr.gov/lc/hooverdam. $8 (parking $7). Tours daily 9:25am $11-$30. All vehicles are subject to inspection; restrictions bar certain vehicles from the dam site.

Spanning the Colorado River at the Arizona-Nevada border, Hoover Dam rises nearly 800ft from Black Canyon below. An incredible feat of civil engineering, the concrete arch-gravity dam began operation in 1936, at a cost $165 million. The project created the largest reservoir in North America, **Lake Mead**, a recreational showpiece. The new Bypass Bridge eases former traffic snarls atop the dam, over which US 93 used to cross the river. A multi-story parking garage on the Nevada side also holds a **visitor center★**, from which there are sensational **views★★** down the front of the dam; presentations focus on the construction, but don't miss the desert flash-flood **demonstration★** (*upstairs*).

🏛 Las Vegas★★★

I-15 and I-515. 31mi northwest of Hoover Dam, in Nevada. Visitor center at 3150 Paradise Rd; 877-847-4858; www.lasvegas.com.

Globally famed for its elaborate casinos, lavish resort hotels, world-class entertainment, lax social ethos and garish character, Las Vegas is without peer on the planet. The metro area has 150,000 hotel rooms, draws 39 million visitors a year and reaps $9 billion annually in gaming revenue.

The Strip★★★
Las Vegas Blvd. South.
This 4.5mi stretch of urban highway *(from the Stratosphere in the north to Mandalay Bay Resort in the south)* holds the greatest concentration of resorts and casinos. Highlights include:
The Venetian★★★ – *3355 Las Vegas Blvd. S. 702-414-1000. www. venetian.com.* Structures replicate Venice, Italy's Doge's Palace, St. Mark's Square, and Rialto Bridge. Gondoliers glide along the **Grand Canal★★**, lined by faux-15C shops.
Bellagio★★★ – *3600 Las Vegas Blvd. S. 702-693-7111. www.bellagio.com.* Twice-hourly light and **fountain shows★★** grace the lake at this opulent complex, designed to recall a village on Italy's Lake Como. The **Bellagio Gallery of Fine Art★★** features rotating exhibits.
Luxor★★ – *3900 Las Vegas Blvd. S. 702-262-4000. www.luxor.com.* A 10-story **sphinx** stands before a 36-story **pyramid**, clad in 13 acres of bronze-tinted glass. "Inclinators" climb to hotel rooms via a shaft angled at 39 degrees.

Touring Tip

To get around, consider taking the **Las Vegas Monorail** (*$5, $12 day pass; 702-699-8299; www. lvmonorail.com*), which runs along the east side of The Strip (*behind hotels, requiring passengers to navigate vast casino floors to reach the train*) from the MGM Grand to the Sahara Hotel. The CityCenter tram runs between the CityCenter, Monte Carlo and Bellagio.

FLAGSTAFF★

Located some 80mi southeast of the Grand Canyon's South Rim, cool, high-country Flagstaff is the region's biggest city. Nearby rise the ancient volcanic San Francisco Peaks, topping out at 12,633ft at Humphreys Peak, Arizona's highest point. Established as a logging and livestock-ranching center, Flagstaff grew as a transportation hub— first for the railroad in 1882, and later for auto travelers on historic Route 66. Today it is home to some 65,000 people; 134,000 in the metro area. Sitting at an elevation of 7,000ft, the city experiences, on average, about 288 days of sunshine and 23 inches of snowfall a year.

Hunter-gatherer groups of Paleo-Indians probably occupied the region as early as 11,000 years ago. Over the centuries, various tribes, including the Hohokam and Sinagua, thrived here. In modern times, the Yavapai and Tonto Apaches made this area their home.

Flagstaff traces its history to 1876, when New England immigrants attached a US flag to the top of a tall, trimmed pine tree to honor their nation on Independence Day. That original **flagstaff** became a trail marker for westbound

travelers. Initial construction in 1880 of the Atlantic and Pacific Railroad from Albuquerque to California would impact the tiny settlement, as would the creation of an area lumber mill. When the tracks reached Flagstaff in 1882, local cattle and sheep ranchers as well as timber barons began using the railroad to ship their products. Local businesses sprang up to service the railroad and its passengers, and Flagstaff began to prosper and grow. The opening in 1899 of Northern Arizona Normal School (now University) cemented the town's future.

In the 1950s and 60s, Flagstaff was a key stop on **Historic Route 66**, the "Mother Road" that ran some 2,000 miles from Chicago to Los Angeles in the days before the

Hotel Monte Vista

©Gwen Cannon/Michelin

Practical Information

When to Go

Flagstaff's weather is delightful May through October, with daily highs in the 60s°F and 70s°F. **Monsoon season** in July and August brings brief thunderstorms. In **winter**, Flagstaff experiences regular snowfalls and sharp cold. Temperatures below zero have been recorded from October through April.

Getting There

♦ **By Air** – US Air provides direct service between Phoenix (PHX) and Flagstaff airport (FLG), with connections in Phoenix to cities throughout North America and around the world.

♦ **By Car** – Flagstaff lies at the junction of Interstate 40 and I-17, 156mi north of Phoenix (2.5hrs) along I-17, 467mi (7.5hrs) east of Los Angeles on I-40; and 251mi (4hrs) east of Las Vegas on US 93 and I-40.

♦ **By Train** – Amtrak's Southwest Chief train serves Flagstaff from Los Angeles and Albuquerque, with one train a day in each direction (www.amtrak.com).

Getting Around

♦ **By Bus** – Mountain Line provides local service in and around Flagstaff on seven routes ($1.25; 928-779-6624; mountainline.az.gov).

♦ **By Taxi** – Service is provided by a half dozen companies; visit www.flagstaffarizona.org for details.

Visitor Information

The main visitor center is located in the Train Depot, 1 E. Rte. 66 at Leroux St. For more information about Flagstaff, call 928-774-9541 or 800-379-0065, or go online to www.flagstaffarizona.org.

---

interstate highway system. A strip of neon motels, mom-and-pop cafes and "last-chance-for-gas" truck stops recalls that era. Today this city is the commercial hub for a huge and sparsely populated area, a gateway to the Grand Canyon, and a very popular summer home site for Phoenix residents who head north to "Flag" in May to escape the heat. Within the boundaries of Coconino County lie the Grand Canyon, Glen Canyon Dam, the city of Sedona, the western third of the Navajo Nation Reservation and three national monuments (Wupatki, Sunset Crater and Walnut Canyon). From Flagstaff's **visitor center**, ensconced in the 1926 Tudor Revival **railway station** (*1 E. Rte. 66 at Leroux St.; 928-774-9541*), walking tours depart for the downtown **historic district**; highlights of the district include the 1889 **Hotel Weatherford** (*23 N. Leroux St.*), with wraparound balconies on its upper floors. At night, the refurbished hotel is magically illuminated.

On New Year's Eve, it's the site of the city's annual **Great Pine Cone Drop** (*see Calendar of Events*), when residents gather to watch a gigantic metal cone be lowered from the hotel's balcony, à la Time Square's ball drop. Also here is the 1927 **Hotel Monte Vista** (*100 N. San Francisco St., see Hotels*), whose construction was partially funded

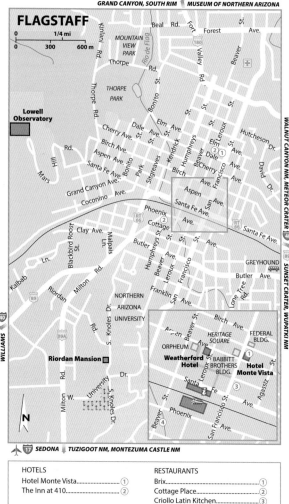

FLAGSTAFF

0   1/4 mi
0   300   600 m

MOUNTAIN VIEW PARK

THORPE PARK

Lowell Observatory

WALNUT CANYON NM, METEOR CRATER

WILLIAMS

SUNSET CRATER, WUPATKI NM

NORTHERN ARIZONA UNIVERSITY

Riordan Mansion

GREYHOUND

ORPHEUM

HERITAGE SQUARE

FEDERAL BLDG.

Weatherford Hotel

BABBITT BROTHERS BLDG.

Hotel Monte Vista

N

HOTELS		RESTAURANTS	
Hotel Monte Vista	①	Brix	①
The Inn at 410	②	Cottage Place	②
		Criollo Latin Kitchen	③
		Macy's European Coffeehouse	④

by the writer **Zane Grey**. Seven sandstone buildings on the **Northern Arizona University** campus (*Kendrick St. & Ellery Ave., south of Butler Ave.; 928-523-9011; www.nau.edu*), built between

1894 and 1935, are listed on the National Register of Historic Places. At more than 17,000 students, NAU has become a major university in the 21C.

MUSEUMS

♦ Museum of Northern Arizona ★

3101 N. Fort Valley Rd.
928-774-5213. www.musnaz.org.
Open year-round daily 9am–5pm.
Closed Jan 1, Thanksgiving Day
& Dec. 25. $10.

Founded in 1928 by zoologist
Harold Colton and his wife, artist
Mary-Russell Ferrell Colton, this
highly regarded museum offers
a comprehensive overview of
the natural surroundings and
human culture of its region.
Well-considered exhibits in 9
galleries depict southwestern
Native American cultures, both
ancient and modern, and offer
an introduction to the geology,
archaeology, anthropology and
arts of northern Arizona.
On view on a rotating basis are
Navajo and Hopi **weavings** as
well as Native American pottery,
jewelry and katsina dolls. A Hopi
mural, **Journey of the Human
Spirit**★, is on permanent display
in the Kiva Gallery.
The museum also offers an
active program of exhibits and
presentations devoted to the
surrounding region, ranging
from documentaries depicting
the Indian fry bread tradition to
displays explaining the impact
of climate change on Northern
Arizona.
The large **museum shop**, with
its extensive Native American
arts and crafts, is one of the best
places to shop for authentic
indigenous items. Among
the merchandise are baskets,
jewelry, pottery, weavings and
katsina dolls.

Museum of Northern Arizona

Michele Mountain © 2011 MNA

Riordan Mansion ★

409 W. Riordan Rd. 928-779-4395;
www.azstateparks.com. Visit by
guided tour only year-round Thu–
Mon 9:30am–5pm. $10.

This 1904 mansion was the home
of two timber-baron brothers,
whose Arizona Lumber and Timber
Co. was a pivotal element in the
area's early 20C development.
The Riordan brothers married two
sisters, and the resulting families
shared this estate. Designed by
Charles Whittlesey, who also
designed Grand Canyon's El Tovar
Hotel, the exterior of the 13,000sq
ft structure features log siding
and volcanic stone arches. Visitors
enter via a whimsical covered
wooden gate★.
Inside the mansion, Arts and Crafts
furniture, period costumes and
home furnishings are on display;
some of the furniture pieces are by
Stickley, Edison, Ellis and Steinway.

FOR KIDS

Lowell Observatory★

1400 W. Mars Hill Rd., 1mi west of downtown Flagstaff. 928-774-3358. www.lowell.edu. Open Jun–Aug daily 9am–10pm. See website for other months. $11, children $4 (ages 5-17).

Astronomer Percival Lowell established this facility in 1894 on a hill near today's downtown Flagstaff. Here in 1930, Clyde Tombaugh discovered Pluto by photographing sections of the night sky at six-day intervals and looking for movements in the minuscule dots of light. Lowell's own 24in Alvan Clark **refracting telescope** is on display and in use during frequent nighttime sky-viewing sessions. Multimedia presentations, hourly tours and evening planetarium shows add opportunities for learning. A **nature trail** through the encircling forest is a great place for kids to stretch their legs.

Clark Telescope, Lowell Observatory

©Tom Alexander/Lowell Observatory

Museum of Northern Arizona★

(see above for location and hours). Children $6 (ages 10-17).

The **Geology Gallery**, with its fossils and dinosaur bones, is a magnet for kids. The **Discovery Room** features games, interactive exhibits and puppet shows.

Slide Rock State Park★

24mi south of Flagstaff (see Oak Creek Canyon below). 928-282-3034. www.azparks.gov. Children under 13 free.

This park is known for its slippery **natural chute** in flatrock through which Oak Creek runs. The **Oak Creek Canyon** spot is a big hit, especially with youngsters. There are also hiking trails, and an apple orchard that was first planted in 1912 by an area homesteader.

Flagstaff Train Station

1 E. Rte. 66 at Leroux St., downtown Flagstaff. 928-774-9541.

Kids can watch Amtrak passenger and Burlington Northern freight trains pass the station with frequent regularity, whistles blaring. The station is very much an active facility, serving more than 100 passengers a day as well as housing the city's visitor center.

Bearizona

I-40 and Rte. 64, 25mi west of Flagstaff. 928-635-2289. bearizona.com. Open year-round daily 8am; closing hrs vary. $20, children $10 (ages 4-12).

MUST DO FLAGSTAFF

Oak Creek Canyon

©Gwen Cannon/Michelin

This drive-through animal park outside Williams will thrill kids with its resident black bears, Dall sheep, wolves, raptors, bison and other mammals.

Grand Canyon Deer Farm

6769 E. Deer Farm Rd., I-40W Exit 171, 25mi west of Flagstaff. 928-635-4073. www.deerfarm.com. Open mid-Mar–mid-Oct daily

9am–6pm. Rest of the year daily 10am–5pm. Closed Thanksgiving and Dec 25. $9.95, children $5.95 (ages 3-13).

Children have opportunities to pet one of the many fallow deer at this large farm, which has been caring for the four-legged animals since 1969. It is also home to miniature donkeys, goats, marmosets and one lone camel.

THE GREAT OUTDOORS

Oak Creek Canyon★★

Take US-89A south 14mi from Flagstaff to Oak Creek Vista to begin a scenic drive. www.oakcreekcanyontaskforce.org.

The two-lane highway is often crowded with traffic. Drivers are cautioned to be patient; passing other vehicles may be difficult or dangerous.
Redwall Limestone, the first stratum of sedimentary rock exposed in the red-rock formations, began to form 330 million years ago when seawater

blanketed the area. The basaltic lava that caps the walls of Oak Creek Canyon was the result of volcanic activity 7 million years ago. **Oak Creek** began cutting its gorge into a fault line about 1 million years ago. Settlers trickled into Oak Creek Canyon after the first homesteader set up housekeeping in 1876, but by 1900 there were only about 20 families in the area. It was afforded special protection by the state in 1991. Today, a lovely 14mi scenic drive descends more than 2,000ft through a steep-walled, 1,200ft-

Ponderosa Pine

Flagstaff is situated within the 1.8 million-acre **Coconino National Forest**, which includes one of the largest contiguous ponderosa pine stands on earth. Found in Arizona largely at elevations of 6,000ft-8,000ft, this handsome conifer is identified by its statuesque form, which can reach well past 200ft in height and 25ft in circumference. Its distinctive reddish bark is thick and deeply furrowed, to fend off fire damage—most old ponderosas bear char marks evidencing past fires. Many trees have a distinct vanilla scent to the bark. The ponderosa's range extends from southern British Columbia in Canada to northern Mexico. Its attractive, strong wood makes it one of the most desirable timber species in the West.

deep canyon, about a mile wide. The main descent begins at **Oak Creek Vista★★** (elevation 6,400ft) with a dramatic 2mi series of switchbacks.

Stunning **views★★** down the gorge encompass forests of ponderosa pine and fir trees crowning the Mogollon Rim. The creek pours over tiers of smooth sandstone at **Slide Rock State Park★** (*8mi north of Sedona; 928-282-3034; www.azparks.gov*), a hugely popular swimming hole on hot summer days. Just outside Sedona, the road skirts the banks of sparkling Oak Creek (elevation 4,300ft), where native ash, cottonwood, sycamore, willow and walnut thrive. To learn more about this unique ecosystem, visit the website shown above.

Coconino National Forest★

US-89A and I-17 south of Flagstaff. (supervisor's office in Flagstaff: 1824 S. Thompson St.). 928-527-3600. www.fs.usda.gov/ coconino. All vehicles must stay on designated roads as shown in the online Motor Vehicle Use Map.

This vast 1.8 million-acre forest stretches from well north of Flagstaff southward past Sedona. It offers plenty of recreation for visitors (*permits required: see the website*), including camping, fishing stocked lakes and streams (even ice-fishing in winter), boating, swimming, picnicking, hiking and horseback riding; as well as winter sports such as skiing and snowshoeing. Its diverse habitat is home to a variety of wildlife such as golden eagles, hawks, falcons, deer, elk, bobcats, foxes, coyotes and other animals. US 89A skirts the **Red Rock Secret Mountain Wilderness** area as it leads south to Sedona. I-17 passes near the **Munds Mountain Wilderness** en route southwest to Camp Verde.

On the slopes of Humphreys Peak, **Arizona Snowbowl★** (*www. arizonasnowbowl.com*) is the state's leading ski resort. With six lifts, 777 acres and a 2,300ft vertical drop, as well as an extensive network of groomed Nordic trails, it is one of the Southwest's most notable ski areas, and usually has reliable snow from mid-December to April (*www.arizonasnowbowl.com*).

EXCURSIONS

Walnut Canyon National Monument★

Walnut Canyon Rd., 3mi south of I-40, 7.5mi east of Flagstaff. 928-526-3367. www.nps.gov/waca. $5.

A set of Sinagua cliff dwellings, occupied from the early 12C to mid-13C, are built into the 350ft-high walls of Walnut Creek canyon. Most ruins are well below the canyon rim, nestled in alcoves in the overhanging rock. The **Island Trail** (*1mi round-trip*) requires a degree of high-altitude fitness, but visitors who descend 185ft (via 240 steps) are rewarded with glimpses of two dozen ancient dwellings.

Sunset Crater Volcano National Monument★

Sunset Crater-Wupatki Rd., east of US-89, 14mi northeast of Flagstaff. 928-526-0502. www.nps.gov/sucr. Visitor center open year-round daily 9am–5pm; closed Dec 25. Trails open dawn–dusk. $5.

A 1,000ft-high cinder cone, which erupted in 1064, is surrounded by hundreds of acres of black lava flows and cinders, out of which sprouts an improbable pine forest. A 1mi loop trail skirts the base of the volcano. You cannot climb Sunset Crater itself, but trails access smaller, nearby cinder cones. The entire volcanic landscape here makes for an eerie, other-worldly experience.

Wupatki National Monument★

Sunset Crater-Wupatki Rd., east of US-89, 33mi northeast of Flagstaff. 928-679-2365. www.nps.gov/wupa. Visitor center open year-round daily 9am–5pm; closed Dec 25. Trails open dawn–dusk. $5.

Pueblo-style masonry ruins are spread across this vast volcanic plain, remains of a Sinagua farming community that lived here 800 years ago. The highlight of the 55sq-mi preserve is the **Wupatki Pueblo**, accessible from an overlook or a paved .5mi (round-trip) trail directly to the rear of the visitor center. The extraordinary site includes a 100-room pueblo, ball court and amphitheater.

©Gwen Cannon/Michelin

Wupatki Pueblo, Wupatki National Monument

NORTH-CENTRAL ARIZONA★★

The 30mi drive south from Flagstaff to Sedona, descending through the forests and famed red-rock scenery of Oak Creek Canyon, is brief but captivating. Sedona has lured artists and other creative types for a century. The mountainside hamlet of Jerome, Western-flavored Williams, and the former Territorial capital of Prescott are other must-see sights in the region. Towering red-rock spires and history-rich Native American sites have long attracted visitors and new residents to these north-central Arizona towns. The region's deciduous riparian woodlands draw many sightseers in autumn to savor the spectacle of the colorful leaves.

CITIES

SEDONA★★

US-89A and Rte. 179. Visitor center at 331 Forest Rd.; 928-282-7722 or 800-288-7336; visitsedona.com.

Sitting at an elevation of 4,500ft, this small city owes its mystique to the variety of striking red buttes and spires that surround it. It is located in the heart of **Red Rock Country★★★**, bounded by Oak Creek and Sycamore Canyons, the Mogollon Rim and Verde Valley. The region takes its name from rust color exposed in three mid-level sandstone strata sculpted between 270 million and 300 million years ago. Founded in 1902, Sedona evolved after World War II into a destination that today is part resort town, part artist colony and part retirement center. Its economy is based largely upon tourism and the arts. The town accommodates some 11,000 permanent residents and attracts about 2.5 million tourists each year.
Maps of the Sedona area identify such landmarks as **Cathedral Rock, Bell Rock** and **Boynton Canyon**. In the 1980s, some of these sites were identified as "vortices," where energy emanates from the earth. Sedona's red rocks have become a beacon for the New Age, attracting visitors seeking spiritual enlightenment. *(Vortex tours are offered by several local enterprises; contact the Sedona Metaphysical Spiritual Association, www.sedonaspiritual.com.)*
To experience Red Rock Country up close, you'll need sturdy hiking boots or a four-wheel-drive vehicle. Several companies provide off-road **Jeep tours** to vista points, vortices, wildflower meadows, Sinagua ruins and other sites. If you are driving yourself, convenient backcountry access is via **Schnebly Hill Road★** *(off Rte. 179, across the Oak Creek bridge from the US-89A "Y" junction).* This 12mi road—pavement gives way to rutted dirt after the first mile—rewards visitors with stunning **views★★★** of red-rock formations and a panorama that spans the valley below.
Sedona's original commercial core is called not "downtown" but **Uptown**. Just north of the "Y" intersection on US-89A, a plethora

of shops and galleries in Old West-style structures offer everything from Native American crafts to New Age items. As you walk along the main street, you'll glimpse famous red rocks named Snoopy and Steamboat. Down the hill off Route 179 sits **Tlaquepaque Arts & Crafts Village** *(see Shopping p84)*, a charming shopping complex modeled after the village of San Pedro de Tlaquepaque in Guadalajara, Mexico.

JEROME★

US-89A, 29mi southwest of Sedona. 928-634-2900. www.jeromechamber.com.

Clinging precariously to the slope of Cleopatra Hill, 2,000ft above the adjacent plain, Jerome began as a rough-and-tumble mining camp in 1876. One of the world's richest veins of copper ore—more than $4 billion worth was extracted—had the community flourishing by the early 20C. In the late 1920s, the population stood at 15,000, but then Jerome went into a steady decline until the last mine closed in 1953. During the 1960s and 70s, Jerome became a haven for artists and others seeking solidarity in the counterculture; figurative arts and handicrafts such as jewelry-making thrive today.

The town now has about 400 residents, 300 historic structures and a handful of restaurants and artisans' galleries along its winding streets. Booklets for self-guided tours are available at the visitor information trolley on Hull Avenue. Just south of the town's center, exhibits at **Jerome State Historic Park★** *(Douglas Rd.; 928-634-5381; www.azparks.gov)* in a 1916 adobe

Touring Tip

Have java, breakfast or lunch in the intimate patio of **Alice's Restaurant** *(403 Clark St., Jerome; 928-634-2069; closed Wed)*, where specialty coffees and teas, chile burros, homemade soups and pies and flat-bread sandwiches are freshly prepared, with local ingredients when available.

mansion built for mine owner "Rawhide Jimmy" Douglas, explore town history.

PRESCOTT★

Off US-89 and Rte. 69. Visitor center at 117 W. Goodwin St. (at Montezuma St.). 928-445-2000 or 800-266-7534; www.visit-prescott. com; map and walking-tour brochure available.

Situated a mile high, the former capital of the Arizona Territory still centers on its historic **Courtyard**

©Gwen Cannon/Michelin

Hotel Connor, Jerome

NORTH-CENTRAL ARIZONA

Plaza★, lined with handsome elm trees. Opposite the plaza's west side, along Montezuma Street, **Whiskey Row** was once filled with saloons. Among them, **The Palace** *(120 S. Montezuma St.)*, whose customers in the 1870s included Wyatt Earp and Doc Holliday, was rebuilt after a fire in 1900 affected 11 blocks. Back then, more high-brow entertainment could be found at the 1905 **Elks Opera House** *(119 E. Gurley St.)*, still in operation as a performing-arts venue today.

Prescott was established in 1864 by Congressional directive, primarily to obtain minerals for the Union side during the Civil War. Mining was the area's chief industry then, also supplying construction materials for town buildings. In 1867 the capital was transferred to Tucson for 10 years, but again returned to Prescott in 1877 until 1889. Today this city of 43,000 residents retains few structures from its founding days, other than the log-sided **Governor's Mansion** *(see Sharlot Hall Museum opposite)*. Anchoring the town square, Yavapai County Courthouse dates to 1916 (the 1878 original did not survive).

Among the many interesting shops around the plaza, **Drawn West** *(134 W. Gurley St.; 928-778-5725)* stocks Western wear and gear, and **Clothes Hound** *(122 S. Montezuma; 928-771-0811)* attracts women with appealing fashions and accessories.

WILLIAMS

I-40 and Rte. 64. Visitor center at 200 W. Railroad Ave.; 928-635-1418; www.experiencewilliams.com.

Sitting at 6,770ft in the Kaibab National Forest, this town of 3,000 was founded in 1880. Once a logging center, today it's associated with **Route 66** *(a 2mi segment nearby can be driven)* and the Grand Canyon Railway. An Old-West feel marks the downtown, where "members" of the Cataract Creek Gang, in full cowboy getup, stage mock **gunfights** on a daily basis. Several shops on the main street sell Native American crafts, **leather goods** (including locally handcrafted saddles) and Route 66 paraphernalia. Every year one of the state's biggest rodeos is held here, the **Cowpunchers Reunion Rodeo** *(See Calendar of Events)*.

Clothes Hound, Prescott

©Gwen Cannon/Michelin

MUSEUMS

🏛 Sharlot Hall Museum★★

415 W. Gurley St., Prescott. 928-445-3122. www.sharlot.org. Open May–Sept Mon–Sat 10am–5pm, Sun noon–4pm. Rest of the year Mon–Sat 10am–4pm, Sun noon–4pm. Closed Jan 1, Thanksgiving Day and Dec 25. $5.

Founded in 1927 by the state's first female territorial historian, for whom the museum is named, this 4-acre complex of 9 buildings serves as a repository of state and local history. Highlights include the original log-sided **Governor's Mansion★★**, erected in 1864. Constructed of locally milled lumber, the **John C. Frémont House★** dates to 1875. The 1880 **Bashford House** shows off fanciful details of Victorian architecture. A fine collection of some 400 **Native American baskets** includes a prized 800-year-old Anasazi creation. Of the gardens on the grounds, the **rose garden** honors Arizona's female pioneers with more than 250 bushes.

Phippen Museum★

4701 S. US-89N., Prescott. 928-778-1385. www.phippenartmuseum.org. Open year-round Tue–Sat 10am–4pm, Sun noon–4pm. Closed Thanksgiving Day and Dec 25. $7.

Opened in 1984, this museum at the edge of town is devoted to 🏛 **Western art**. Its permanent collection of paintings, bronze sculptures, photographs and Native American artifacts date from the late 1800s to the present.

The Phippen is the repository for personal memorabilia and works by 19C sculptor **Solon Borglum**, brother of famed Mount Rushmore sculptor, Gutzon Borglum.

Smoki Museum★

14701 N Arizona Ave., Prescott. 928-445-1230. www.smoki museum.org. Open year-round Mon–Sat 10am–4pm, Sun 1pm–4pm. Closed Easter, Thanksgiving Day, Dec 25 and Dec 31. $5.

A stone replica of a Hopi Pueblo dwelling, built in 1935, holds this museum showcasing Southwest indigenous arts, crafts and artifacts. Inside, some of the museum walls feature kachina paintings. Of special interest are Apache, Sioux and Woodland Indians' ceremonial accoutrements, as well as a large number of baskets made by the local Yavapai and other tribes.

Phippen Museum

©Gwen Cannon/Michelin

SHOPPING

Exposures International Gallery of Fine Art

561 Rte. 179, Sedona. 928-282-1125. www.exposuresfineart.com.

This enormous store has a sizable inventory of fine and decorative art. Inside are stone and bronze water fountains, exquisite photographs of red-rock country and other content, handcrafted jewelry, and glass works in myriad designs. Many pieces from the gallery's large assemblage of bronze sculptures are displayed outside in the on-site garden.

Hummingbird House

100 Brewer Rd., Sedona. 928-282-0705.

Housed in a general store built in 1926, this charming shop purveys custom–made furniture as well as antiques, jewelry, greeting cards, linens and specialty seasonal

items, many produced by Sedona artists. The store maintains a second location in the Hyatt Shops at Piñon Pointe.

Hyatt Shops at Piñon Pointe

US-89A and Rte. 179, Sedona. 928-254-1006. www.theshopsat hyattpinonpointe.com.

Spreading along a hillside backed by red-rock formations, this modern Pueblo-style complex was sited with views in mind. Stores and restaurants surround spacious courtyards adorned with native plants and boulders. Shops selling men's clothing, women's apparel, fine jewelry, wine and works of art share the space with Wildflower Bread Company, Cold Stone Creamery and Starbucks.

Tlaquepaque Arts & Crafts Village

336 Rte. 179 at the bridge, Sedona. 928-282-4838. www.tlaq.com.

Planted with a profusion of colorful flowers and plants and shaded by venerable sycamore trees, this expansive Mexican-style "village" makes a pleasant spot to stroll in fountain-topped courtyards, narrow passageways and tiled plazas. The delightful setting and more than 45 shops, art galleries and restaurants have made Tlaquepaque a popular destination for Sedona visitors as well as local residents. Specialty stores include those selling music boxes, toys, jewelry and rugs, and the elegant restaurant **René** makes its home here *(see Restaurants)*.

Tlaquepaque Arts & Crafts Village

©Gwen Cannon/Michelin

EXCURSIONS

Chapel of the Holy Cross★

End of Chapel Rd. off Rte. 179, 7mi south of uptown Sedona. 928-284-3129 or 888-242-7359. www.chapeloftheholycross.com.

This Roman Catholic chapel was completed in 1956 (Anshen & Allen), the brainchild of local artist and rancher Marguerite Brunswig Staude. Characterized by its cruciform shape, the concrete aggregate-and-glass chapel rises 90ft from the base of a red-rock butte.

Montezuma Castle National Monument★

Montezuma Rd., Camp Verde, 1mi east of I-17, Exit 289. 928-567-3322. www.nps.gov/moca.

Impossibly tucked into a natural limestone alcove 50-100ft above the floor of Beaver Creek, this 5-story, 20-room "castle" was part of a larger early 12C Sinaguan community. Though the dwelling was not intended as a fortress, its location protected its occupants from the elements, and supplied natural insulation against heat and cold, without taking up valuable farmland.

Tuzigoot National Monument★

Tuzigoot Rd. off Rte. 279, Clarkdale; 23mi southwest of Sedona via US-89A to Cottonwood. 928-634-5564. www.nps.gov/tuzi.

Occupied from 1000 to 1400 AD, this ancient Sinagua pueblo tops a ridge 120ft above the Verde River.

At its height in the late 1300s, Tuzigoot (Apache for "crooked water") was home to about 225 people, who lived in 86 ground-floor rooms and perhaps 15 second-story rooms, and farmed the fertile valley. Visitors, following a gently sloping .25mi trail, may enter several rooms. Artifacts in the visitor center help interpret cultural practices.

Granite Dells★

4mi northeast of downtown Prescott, off US-89A. Accessible from Watson Lake Park, 3101 Watson Lake Rd.; 928-777-1121.

Granite boulders of all shapes and sizes surround **Watson Lake**. The 1mi **Discovery Trail** traces the lakeshore, and the 4mi gravel **Prescott Peavine National Recreation Trail** appeals to bikers, horseback riders and hikers.

Arcosanti

34mi southeast of Prescott via Rte. 69 (or I-17, Exit 262) in Cordes Junction. 928-533-6295; www.arcosanti.org. Tours year-round daily 9am–5pm. Closed major holidays. $10 donation.

This complex is still a work in progress. Based on principles first articulated by Italian architect **Paolo Soleri** in 1963, construction at the site was begun in 1970. The 25-acre community is designed to represent a "lean alternative" to modern cities, with an emphasis on providing equitable access to urban amenities. His sister community is Cosanti *(see PHOENIX)*.

PHOENIX★★

To some, Southern Arizona's Sonoran Desert is brutal. Its average annual rainfall is less than 10 inches, and temperatures often exceed 100ºF. Saguaro cactus, some 40ft tall, mark this land as an alien climate for most visitors. But others find heaven here. A brief, sudden thunderstorm can cause the desert to erupt in color—the ocotillo blossom's flaming orange, the palo verde's yellow, the prickly pear's peach, the saguaro's dazzling ivory. Sprawling Phoenix, sixth-largest city in the US, is located in the very heart of this desert.

Fast Facts

Land area: 517 sq mi

Population: 1.5 million

Record temperatures: hottest 122˚F (June 26, 1990); coldest 16˚F (Jan. 7, 1913)

Average annual precipitation: 7.66 inches

Golf courses: more than 200 in Greater Phoenix

Professional sports: all 4 major leagues play in the Greater Phoenix area

A mid-1860s hay camp built atop a Hohokam site was dubbed "Phoenix," intimating that a new city might rise from ancient ruins just as the mythical bird rose from its ashes. A town site was laid out in 1870. By the end of that decade, the village was a supply center for central Arizona mines and ranches; and in 1889 it was named **territorial capital**. Its transition from frontier town was assured in 1911, one year before Arizona became the 48th US state, when the Salado (Salt) River was dammed 60mi east of Phoenix. Phoenix became Arizona's first **state capital** in 1912, and remains the seat of State government today. Roosevelt Dam and Theodore Roosevelt Lake fostered growth. The Southern Pacific Railroad arrived in 1926. Chewing-gum magnate William Wrigley Jr., industrialist Cornelius Vanderbilt Jr. and famed architect **Frank Lloyd Wright** established second homes in the area, beginning a boom that

Downtown Phoenix

©Greater Phoenix CVB

Practical Information

When to Go

Summer heat (100°F+) abates late Sept-early Oct, which are relatively hot, but low humidity and moderate overnight temperatures make the days pleasant. Temperatures fall through January, when the average is 65°F. **Winter** days are generally mild, but night lows can be in the 30s Dec-Jan. Occasional high 20s in higher elevations around Phoenix are not unheard of. Temperatures begin to rise then, reaching an average high of 102°F in June.

Getting Around

◆ From the Airport – The main airport is **Phoenix Sky Harbor International Airport** (PHX) *(602-273-3300; www.skyharbor.com)*, off I-10, 5min south of downtown.
Light Rail: METRO Light Rail provides access to Sky Harbor via a free shuttle bus that connects with the METRO line at the 44th St. and the Washington stop.
SuperShuttle: 602-244-9000; 800-258-3826; www.supershuttle.com.
Taxi: Three companies serve Sky Harbor: **Apache Taxi** *(480-557-7000)*, **AAA/Yellow Cab** *(480-888-8888)*, and **Mayflower Cab** *(602-955-1355)*. Rates are $5 for first mile; each additional mile $2.30. Traffic delays cost $23/hr. Minimum fare is $15; $1 surcharge per airport trip. www.skyharbor.com.
Car Rental: The Rental Car Center lies near Sky Harbor *(1805 E. Sky Harbor Circle S., between 16th and 24th Sts., south of Buckeye Rd.)* Rental car **shuttle buses** take passengers from the airport to the center. City

of Phoenix Rental Car Information Desk: 602-683-3741.
◆ By Public Transportation
METRO Light Rail: METRO Light Rail is a 20mi light-rail system that runs north and south through central Phoenix and links the city with Mesa and Tempe. For fares and schedules, 602-253-5000; www.valleymetro.org/metrolightrail.
Bus: Valley Metro provides bus service for Metropolitan Phoenix 365 days a year. For fares and routes, 602-253-5000; www.valleymetro.org/vm. Downtown Phoenix Partnership runs Downtown Evening Express, a free **shuttle bus** that connects downtown hotels, attractions and night spots Thu 7pm-11 pm and Fri-Sat 7pm-2 am. 602-254-8696; www.downtownphoenix.com.
◆ By Car – Major expressways are I-10 (Papago Freeway) running east and west in central Phoenix; I-17 (Black Canyon Freeway), which runs north and south on city center's west side; Highway 51 (Piestewa Freeway), heading north and south on the east side; and Highway 101 (Pima Freeway), running north and south on the city's far east side before looping back to connect with I-17 on the northwest corner. Rush-hour traffic is heavy, but especially 6am-9am and 4pm-6pm.

Visitor Information

Downtown Visitor Center *(125 N. 2nd St., across from Hyatt Regency Phoenix Hotel)* is open Mon-Fri 8am-5pm. Also City North Visitor Center *(5415 E. High St., Ste. 121)* is open Fri-Sun 10am-6pm. For information, 602-254-6500.

PHOENIX

Desert Botanical Garden

©DBG, Adam Rodriquez/Greater Phoenix CVB

continues to the present. Today the capital city has more major **golf and spa resorts** than anywhere else between Florida and Southern California. Ringed by the Superstition Mountains to the east, the White Tank Mountains to the west, South Mountain and the Sierra Estrella to the south and west, and the McDowell Mountains to the north and east, Phoenix is plagued by smog and an occasional dust storm, but it continues to attract new residents as well as some 13-15 million visitors annually.

Downtown consists of 90 square blocks stretching from 3rd Avenue to 7th Street and Fillmore to south of Jackson Street. The main streets are laid parallel in one mile-by-one mile grids, making orientation and navigation simple. **Central Avenue** is the dividing line for north-south streets, which begin east of Central with 1st St. and ascend in number. Avenues run north to south to the west of Central, beginning with 1st Ave. East-west streets are named for US Presidents, but not in order of terms in office. Except for the **Arizona Center** *(see Shopping)* shopping plaza, tree shade is scarce downtown. The city's hub is **Patriots Square**, flanked by Washington and Jefferson Sts., and on its east by Central Avenue. A billion-dollar revitalization has made **Civic Plaza** a major cultural center, home to **Phoenix Symphony Hall** and **Herberger Theater** *(see Performing Arts)*. A major destination for conventions, Phoenix boasts three huge convention centers downtown.

Touring Tip

The Downtown Phoenix Partnership sponsors the **Downtown Phoenix Ambassadors**. On duty 365 days a year *(8am–11pm)*, the ambassadors provide directions, restaurant recommendations, tips on parking and getting around town, as well as guided **walking tours**. Wearing orange shirts, they are a familiar presence on the downtown streets. They can also be found at their **information center** in the US Bank building on Adams St. between 1st and Central Aves. 602-495-1500.

PHOENIX

0		4 mi
0		6 km

MUSICAL INSTRUMENT MUSEUM

ADOBE DAM REG. PARK

Phoenix Deer Valley

PARADISE VALLEY

PARADISE VALLEY MALL

SCOTTSDALE

Scottsdale Municipal

NORTH MTN. PARK

METROCENTER

SUNNYSLOPE

GLENDALE

GRAND CANYON UNIV.

PHOENIX MOUNTAINS PARK AND REC. AREA

PARADISE VALLEY

SALT RIVER INDIAN RES.

BILTMORE FASHION PARK

HEARD MUSEUM

Phoenix Art Museum

Tovrea Castle

Desert Botanical Garden

Pueblo Grande Museum

PAPAGO PARK

Zoo

DOWNTOWN

Arizona Capitol Museum

Phoenix Sky Harbor International

Hall of Flame Fire Museum

SUN DEVIL STADIUM

ARIZONA STATE UNIVERSITY

TEMPE DIABLO STADIUM

TEMPE

SOUTH MOUNTAIN

GUADALUPE

Mystery Castle

Dobbins Lookout

SOUTH MOUNTAIN PARK/PRESERVE

AHWATUKEE FOOTHILLS

GILA RIVER INDIAN RESERVATION

CHANDLER

APACHE JUNCTION

FLAGSTAFF

TUCSON

N

Street/Road labels

Pinnacle Peak Rd., Pima Fwy., Cave Creek Rd., Deer Valley Rd., Union Hills Dr., Bell Rd., Greenway Rd., Thunderbird Rd., Peoria Ave., Dunlap Ave., Northern Ave., Glendale Ave., Camelback Rd., Indian School Rd., Thomas Rd., McDowell Rd., Van Buren Rd., Buckeye Rd., Maricopa Fwy., Broadway Rd., Baseline Rd., Dobbins Rd., Chandler Blvd., Pecos Rd., Tatum Blvd., Scottsdale Rd., Frank Lloyd Wright Blvd., Cactus Rd., Shea Blvd., Lincoln Dr., Indian Bend Rd., McDonald Dr., Hayden Rd., Pima Rd., Main St., Guadalupe Rd., Elliot Rd., Warner Rd., Ray Rd., McClintock Dr., Price Fwy., Dobson Rd., Rural Rd., Mill Ave., 7th Ave., 7th St., 19th Ave., 35th Ave., 43rd Ave., 24th St., 32nd St., 44th St., 56th St., Black Canyon Fwy., Piestewa Fwy., Lori, Grand Ave.

PHOENIX

HISTORICAL SITES

Heritage and Science Park

Bounded by N. 5th, N. 7th, E. Washington and E. Monroe Sts.

This park houses the **Arizona Science Center** *(see For Fun).* A few blocks west, the **Orpheum Theatre** *(203 W. Adams St.),* built in Spanish Colonial Revival style in 1929, was recently restored.

Heritage Square

Between E. Monroe and E. Adams, N. 5th and N 7th Sts. 602-262-5071. www.phoenix.gov/parks.

Of the Phoenix townsite houses built 1895–1902, the 1895 **Rosson House** is the oldest *(see opposite).*

Tovrea Castle at Carraro Heights

5025 E. Van Buren St. 602-256-3221. www.tovreacastletours.com. Guided tours (2hrs) Fri–Sun 8:30am and 11:30am; reservations required. $15.

This landmark topping a small hill just east of downtown looks like a tiered wedding cake. The "castle" was built by an Italian immigrant in 1930, who envisioned it as the centerpiece of a resort.
The resort never materialized, and in 1932, the hotel was sold to businessman E.A. Tovrea. A private society now maintains the castle. In the main floor, fanciful wall and ceiling decorations can be viewed; a large wall mirror is original to the property. About 1,400 cacti fill the 44-acre **cactus garden**.

Rosson House

113 N. 6th St. 602-262-5070; www.rossonhousemuseum.org. Guided tours (1hr) Wed–Sat 10am–4pm, Sun noon–4pm. Closed major holidays. $7.50.

Built in 1895 in the Eastlake style for Dr. and Mrs. Roland Lee Rosson, this Victorian house still stands in its original location downtown in **Heritage Square** *(see above).* Tours of the 2,800sq ft dwelling's 10 rooms afford visitors a glimpse of life in territorial Arizona at the turn of the 19C.

Orpheum Theatre

ORPHEUM

MUSEUMS

🏛 The Heard Museum★★★

2301 N. Central Ave. 602-252-8848. www.heard.org. Open year-round Mon–Sat 9:30am–5pm, Sun 11am–5pm. Closed Dec 25. $18.

Devoted to Native American culture and art, this outstanding museum contains nearly 40,000 works of art displayed in changing and permanent exhibits in 10 galleries. Arches and colonnades are hallmarks of its Spanish Colonial buildings, set around an intimate courtyard. A smaller, satellite museum is located in Scottsdale. The story of its 1929 founding is told in the **Sandra Day O'Connor Gallery**. The permanent exhibit **Home: Native People in the Southwest** displays some 2,000 treasures from collections arranged per major Native groups. At its entry is a 30ft-long, 8ft-high ceramic and glass sculpture of an "art fence" by two Pueblo artists titled **Indigenous Evolution**. Showcased in rotating exhibits are hundreds of hand-carved Hopi **Katsina dolls★★**, including

Katsina dolls

A Hopi katsina (*kat-SEE-na; katchina in English*) made by a well-known carver can fetch $10,000, although the average price ranges from $500 up. Originally carved by Hopi men and given to their female children to ensure fertility, these dolls (*tihu* to the Hopi) represent spirits who intercede with the gods in the growing season. Children are given katsinas, not as toys, but to inspire spiritual values. Hopi religion forbids certain dolls to be produced for anyone outside the tribe. But many other figures, such as **Mud Head Clown** and **Morning Katsina**, are found in museums and shops around the state. No katsina is considered authentic unless it is carved from the root of a **cottonwood tree**, is anatomically correct and bears the artist's signature.

a collection donated by former Senator Barry Goldwater.

"Indigenous Evolution" by Rosemary Lonewolf (Santa Clara Pueblo) and Tony Jojola (Isleta Pueblo).

©Craig Smith

Remembering Our Indian School Days★★ depicts the boarding schools American Indian children were forced to attend. The **Heard Museum Shop** features high-quality jewelry, weavings, artwork, baskets and katsina dolls created by Native American artists, as well as a large selection of books on American Indian art and history. The **Berlin Gallery at the Heard Museum Shop** is an upscale retail gallery that showcases the work of some three-dozen American Indian artists. The on-site **Courtyard Café** (*open daily 11am–3pm*) spotlights recipes that use local ingredients and reflect the culture of the Southwest. Menu items range from fresh salads to fish tacos, and hummus made from tepary beans native to the Sonoran Desert.

Musical Instrument Museum★★★

4725 E. Mayo Blvd. 480-478-6000. www.mim.org. Open year-round Mon–Sat 9am–5pm (Thu–Fri 9pm), Sun 10am–5pm. $18.

Opened in 2010, this stellar museum boasts a collection of some 15,000 musical instruments from around the world. It was the brainchild of Target's former CEO Robert J. Ulrich, an art collector and aficionado of global music. Inside the light-filled 200,000sq ft building, familiar as well as little-known instruments are grouped over two floors according to seven regions of the world and exhibited with **native costumes** and cultural artifacts. Visitors don headsets as they tour to listen to audio recordings; video monitors are stationed throughout to show the instruments actually being played. Among the many highlights are an **18C viola**, an *adufe* from Spain, a Kenyan lyre, West African drums called *djembes* and John Lennon's upright piano.

Phoenix Art Museum★★

1625 N. Central Ave. 602-257-1222. www.phxart.org. Open Wed–Sat 10am–5pm (Wed 9pm), Sun noon –5pm. Closed Thanksgiving Day and Dec 25. $15.

This august museum focuses on American art of the 19C–20C, Western Americana, European art, as well as Latin American art by Rivera, Tamayo, Orozco and Kahlo. Not surprisingly, there is a strong

Musical Instrument Museum

Upper Gallery, Phoenix Art Museum

©Bill Timmerman

emphasis on **Western American Art,** with a collection that includes some 900 paintings, sculptures and works on paper. The museum's extensive modern collection includes works by Picasso, Stella, Rothko and De Kooning.

An **orientation theater** introduces the 17,000-work collection, which includes a reproduction of Gilbert Stuart's 1796 portrait, **George Washington**, pictured on the $1 bill. Frederic Remington's muscular sculpture **Mountain Man** captures the rugged pluck of the men who tamed the Wild West, while Georgia O'Keefe's **Canyon Country** gives a taste of the region's subtle beauty. An innovative collaboration with Tucson's **Center for Creative Photography** brings the works of Ansel Adams, Edward Weston, Richard Avedon, and other celebrated photographers to Phoenix in an ongoing series of exhibitions.

Arizona Capitol Museum

1700 W. Washington St. 602-926-3620. www.lib.az.us/museum. Open year-round Mon–Fri 9am–4pm. Also Sat 10am–2pm Sept–May. Closed state holidays.

Built in 1901, this tuff-and-granite structure served first as the territorial capitol, and became the state capitol when Arizona was admitted to the Union in 1912. Displays inside include artifacts from the *USS Arizona*, sunk at Pearl Harbor in 1941. Edward Curtis, a photographer who traveled extensively among the Indian tribes of Arizona in the early 20C, is celebrated by an extensive collection of his photographs, as well as baskets, pottery and other artifacts that he collected during his journeys.

Pueblo Grande Museum and Archaeological Park

4619 E. Washington St. 602-495-0901. www.pueblogrande.com. Open year-round Mon–Sat 9am–4:45pm, Sun 1pm–4:45pm. $6.

In the 14C, 1,000 people lived at this **Hohokam site** beside the head gate of the canal system. Storage rooms, cemeteries and ball courts are discernible at this National Historic Landmark. Located inside the complex are a **hands-on gallery** for children and a theater where visitors can watch an introductory video about the site and its ⚒ **history**.

MUSEUMS

PARKS AND GARDENS

Desert Botanical Garden★★

1201 N. Galvin Pkwy., Papago Park. 480-941-1225. www.dbg.org. Open year-round daily 8am–8pm. $18.

Hosting more than 20,000 desert plants, this arid-land arboretum has won awards for environmental education. Largely staffed by volunteers who have themselves fallen under the spell of the Sonoran Desert, the lovely garden covers some 145 acres.
Displays include Indian and Hispanic residents' use of **native plants**. Trails snake past cacti and succulents, regional plants and animals. The **walking paths**, which wind through the otherworldly rock formations of **Papago Park** *(opposite)*, have been landscaped to highlight different aspects of the Sonoran environment, including a **wildflower loop**, a path through an **agave yucca forest**, and a desert nature loop lined with stands of towering **organ pipe cactus**. The garden also serves as the backdrop for numerous events including concerts, plant sales and celebrations with an emphasis on Southwest traditions.

Papago Park★

1201 N. Galvin Pkwy. 602-262-6862. www.phoenix.gov/parks. Open year-round daily 5am–7pm.

Southeast Phoenix, between Scottsdale and Tempe, north of the Salt (Salado) River, is dominated by this vast 1,200-acre park, which presents one of the most visually distinctive landscapes in all of Phoenix. It is home to the **Desert Botanical Garden**.
Spanish explorers in the 16C, finding remains of a Hohokam civilization at **Pueblo Grande** *(see Museums)*, labeled these vanished desert farmers *papago*, or "bean eaters." The Hohokam left a complex system of aqueducts among the buttes.
Today people flock to this park to enjoy the outdoors, and to visit one of the city's favorite gardens.

South Mountain Park Preserve★

10919 S. Central Ave. 602-262-7393. www.phoenix.gov/parks. Open year-round daily 5am–7pm.

The 16,500-acre South Mountain Park and Preserve is said to be the largest municipal park in the world. From **Dobbins Lookout**, as well as from trails for hiking, biking and riding, the park offers dramatic city **views**.
At the foot of the mountain sits **Mystery Castle** *(800 E. Mineral Rd., end of S. 7th St., south of Baseline; 602-268-1581)*, an 8,000sq-ft manse hand-built from 1930 to 1945 out of everything from desert rocks to Bing Crosby's golf club.

Barrel cactus

©Joyce Holly/Michelin

FOR KIDS

Arizona Science Center★

600 E. Washington St. 602-716-2000. www.azscience.org. Open year-round daily 10am–5pm. Closed Thanksgiving Day and Dec 25. $14, children $11 (ages 3-17).

This concrete monolithic building (1997, Antoine Predock) holds 300 hands-on exhibits, a 5-story IMAX theater and a cutting-edge planetarium. The exhibit **Forces of Nature** focuses on geology and hydrology. **My Digital World** explores how today's digital communications work.

Chase Field★

401 E. Jefferson St. 602-462-6500. www.arizonadiamondbacks.com. Tours Mon–Sat 9:30am, 11am and 12:30pm. $7, children $3 (ages 4-6).

Opened in 1998, this huge air-conditioned baseball stadium has a retractable roof, and a centerfield **swimming pool** (415ft away from home plate), where home runs make a big splash. "The Bob," as locals know it, is home to Major League Baseball team called the **Arizona Diamondbacks**. With its distinctive natural grass and dirt **walkway** connecting home plate to the pitcher's mound, Chase Field calls to mind ballparks of an earlier era, yet with its retractable roof and the state-of-the-art 136ft-by-46ft High Definition **scoreboard**, Chase dazzles fans with the immersive spectacle expected in contemporary sporting events.

🐾 Phoenix Zoo★

455 N. Galvin Pkwy., Papago Park. 602-273-1341. www.phoenixzoo.org. Open mid-Jan–May daily 9am–5pm, Jun–Aug daily 7am–2pm, early Nov–early Jan daily 9am–4pm. Closed Dec 25. $20. Children $10 (ages 3-12).

White rhinos, Sumatran tigers, South American spectacled bears and a breeding colony of Arabian oryxes are among the zoo's 150 endangered animals. A motorized **Safari Train** runs through the four habitats in which 1,300 animals reside. The **Forest of Uco** simulates a Colombian rain forest. **Arizona Trail** leads to a desert home for coyotes, Mexican wolves and other Southwest wildlife.

Hall of Flame Fire Museum

6101 E. Van Buren St., Papago Park. 602-275-3473. www.hallofflame.org. Open Mon–Sat 9am–5pm, Sun noon–4pm. Closed Jan 1, Thanksgiving Day and Dec 25. $6, children $4 (ages 6-17), $1.50 (ages 3-5).

Retired firefighters share tales of their profession as visitors operate alarms and see fully restored **fire engines** dating back to 1725. Covering almost an entire acre, this museum tells the history of fire fighting through the years with exhibits in 6 galleries that feature more than 90 fully restored pieces of fire-fighting **equipment** and an extensive library devoted to firefighting history and lore. Be sure to see the marvelous collection of historic **helmets**.

OUTDOOR FUN

⛳ Golf

With more than 200 courses in Greater Phoenix, you're sure to get a desirable tee time, especially if you reserve online; but book far in advance for winter and spring rounds. Here's a selection of courses independent of resorts; resort fairways are listed below.

Cave Creek Golf Course
15202 N 19th Ave. 602-866-8076. www.phoenix.gov/recreation.
The most popular municipal golf course in Phoenix, Cave Creek features 18 holes on wide, rolling fairways. Par 72.
Greens Fees: Winter $43. Spring $30. Summer $16. Fall $34.

Foothills Golf Club
2201 E. Clubhouse Dr. 480-460-4653. www.thefoothillsgc.com.
Designed by Tom Weiskopf and Jay Morrish, this par-72 links-style course has earned a top ranking from *Golf Digest*. Rates vary by season and are set every year. 2012 rates ranged from $100 in winter to $50 in summer. Call for 2013 rates.

Grayhawk Golf Club
8620 E. Thompson Peak Pkwy., Scottsdale. 480-502-1800. www.grayhawkgolf.com.
The par-72 Raptor course was designed by Tom Fazio, and *Golf Magazine* has rated it one of the "Top 100 You Can Play in the U.S." Designed by David Graham and Gary Panks, the Talon Course was built around a series of **box canyons** and set amid stands of mesquite, palo verde and ironwood trees. Rates vary by season and day, with Mon–Thu rates as follows: mid-Sep–end Sept $95; Oct–Nov 1 $155; Nov 2–Dec 2 $180; Dec 3–Jan 13 $180.

Papago Golf Course
5595 E Moreland St., 602-275-8428, www.papagogolfcourse.net.
This 18-hole, par-72 course was designed by William Francis (Billy) Bell, who also designed the prestigious Torrey Pines course in San Diego. Rates vary by season and time of day. Call, or go online, for current rates.

Papago Golf Course

MUST DO PHOENIX

We-Ko-Pa Golf Club
18200 E. Toh Vee Circle, Fort McDowell. 480-836-9000. www.wekopa.com.
With two separate 18-hole courses, We-Ko-Pa is located in the Fort McDowell Yavapai Nation, just east of Scottsdale. Stunning desert vistas contribute to a unique golfing experience. Pars 71 and 72. **Rates**: Aug 31–Oct 7 $90; Oct 19–Nov 1 $105; Nov 2–Dec 24 $160; Dec 26–Jan 10 $185; Jan 11–Apr 7 $225.

Golfing the Resorts
Along with the spas, swimming and dining, golf is a mainstay of the Arizona resort experience. Fairways are verdant, despite the arid terrain. **Troon North** is probably the most storied name in Arizona golfing; guests at **Four Seasons Resort Scottsdale at Troon North** (*480-515-5700; www.fourseasons.com/Scottsdale*) are granted special privileges at this legendary golf club. The **Wildfire Golf Club** at **JW Marriott Phoenix Desert Ridge Resort and Spa** (*480-293-5000; www.jwdesertridgeresort.com*) features two 18-hole courses, the Faldo Championship Course and Palmer Signature Course. Golfing at the **Arizona Grand Golf Course** is one of the highlights of any stay at the **Arizona Grand Resort and Spa** (*602-438-9000; www.arizonagrandresort.com*). This challenging par-71 course features dramatic changes in elevation and a links-style layout. The **Arizona Biltmore** (*602-955-6600; www.arizonabiltmore.com*) is one of Arizona's grand old resorts, and its golf course, **The Adobe**, is every bit as grand as the resort itself.

Miniature Golf

Sure, you'll get your time on the links, but what about the kids? **Castles~n~Coasters** (*9445 North Metro Pkwy. East; 602-997-7575; www.castlesncoasters.com*) has long been a local landmark familiar to motorists driving north on I-17. This pint-size amusement complex, with its four 18-hole courses, is a mecca for those who prefer their golf small.

Lush and spacious, the 50-year-old fairways evoke an earlier, more relaxing era in the sport's history.

Hiking

Camelback Mountain
5950 N. Echo Canyon Pkwy. 602-261-8313. www.phoenix.gov/recreation.
Here, find a strenuous 1.2mi ascent of the 2,704ft mountain, or shorter, easier trails in **Echo Canyon**.

Papago Park
625 N Galvin Pkwy. 602-261-8318. www.phoenix.gov/recreation.
The park's trails are smooth and family-friendly, with little variation in elevation. Four trails range from .1mi to 4mi in length.

Piestewa Peak and Dreamy Draw Recreation Area
2701 Squaw Peak Dr. 602-261-8318. www.phoenix.gov/recreation.
Visitors have access to a variety of undeveloped desert habits surrounding 2,608ft Piestewa Peak. Trails rank from easy to difficult, with the 1.2 mi Summit Trail (elevation 2,608ft-1,400ft) and the 4.8 mi Perl Charles Memorial Trail

(elevation 2,200ft-1,340ft) being two of the most strenuous.

South Mountain

10919 S. Central Ave. 602-262-7393. www.phoenix.gov/recreation.
This massif dominates metro Phoenix's southern reaches. On its 51mi of primary **trails**, hikers will see native Sonoran plants and wildlife while enjoying spectacular views of the city below. On **Silent Sundays**, generally held the fourth Sunday of the month, motorized vehicles are banned.

🚣 Kayaking

Saguaro Lake Ranch

13020 N. Bush Hwy., in Mesa. 480-984-2194. www.saguarolakeranch. com. Take Beeline Hwy. (Rte. 87) north 10mi past Shea Blvd., turn south on the Bush Hwy., then 5mi, turn left at the sign for the ranch.
Paddle on Saguaro Lake or the Salt River in a "sit-on-top" kayak *(2hrs $38)*; expect to see wildlife, and to get wet.

🐎 Riding

Ponderosa Stables

10215 S. Central Ave. 602-268-1261.www.arizona-horses.com.
Get a **view** of downtown Phoenix on some of the trails in vast South Mountain Park. The sunset ride pauses for a chow-down at a local steakhouse before sauntering back to the stables under the stars.

Bumble Bee Ranch

50mi north of Phoenix. Exit 248 off I-17, Mile Marker 5. 23925 S. Bumble Bee Ranch Rd. 623-374-0002. www.bumblebeeranch.com.
Take a **trail ride** *(must be 7 years or older; 1hr $42, children under 15 years $27; 2hrs $62, children $42)* amid cottonwood trees along **Bumble Bee Creek** to the foothills of Bradshaw Mountain before returning to the barn. For a real adventure, saddle up for a 2hr-3hr 🐎 **cattle drive** *($100; must be 10 years or older)* through the upper Sonoran Desert. End the day with cowboy grub that has all the fixins *(advance reservations required)*.

Saguaro Lake Ranch

For location and directions, see Kayaking above. Oct–May 1. 480-984-0335. www.saguarolaket railrides.com.
Enjoy a desert **trail ride** *(must be 8 years or older; 1.5hrs $55, children 8-12 years $50; 2hrs $65, children 8-12 years $60)* within Tonto National Forest, fording the **Salt River** and back-dropped by the stunning Superstition Mountains.

Kayaking on Saguaro Lake

©Saguaro Lake Guest Ranch

MUST DO PHOENIX

PERFORMING ARTS

ASU Gammage Auditorium

1200 S. Forest Ave., Tempe. 480-965 -3434. www.asugammage.com.

Designed by renowned architect Frank Lloyd Wright and completed in 1964, this 3,000-seat venue, shaped like a layer cake, soars 80ft high. Performances include touring Broadway shows, operas, symphony concerts and live productions.

Herberger Theater

222 E. Monroe St. 602-254-7399. www.herbergertheater.org.

With three stages and 1,245 seats combined, the multi-level center led the revitalization of downtown when it was built in 1989. Now it's home to the Arizona Theater Company, Actors Theater, and Center Dance Ensemble. It also hosts Childsplay, Arizona Jewish Theatre Company, and The Black Theatre Troupe.

Phoenix Theatre

100 E. McDowell Rd. 602-254-2151. www.phoenixtheatre.com.

Founded in 1920, the organization made a permanent home in this former coach house in 1924. The structure has since been completely rebuilt, and remains a local favorite for community first-run theater and musical performances, alternative and experimental theatre. It hosts the Phoenix Theatre Cookie Company children's group alongside world-recognized productions.

Symphony Hall

75 N. 2nd St. 602-495-1999. www. phoenixconventioncenter.com/ venues/symphony-hall.

All 2,312 seats offer unobstructed views of performances by its resident Phoenix Symphony, Ballet Arizona and Arizona Opera, plus many visiting Broadway theater productions. Built in 1972, the venue was extensively renovated in 2004, and now showcases an art collection that includes the largest piece of machine-crafted embroidery in the world.

Scottsdale Center for the Performing Arts

7380 E. 2nd St., Scottsdale. 480-499-8587. www.scottsdale performingarts.org.

Comprised of the 853-seat Piper Theater/Stage 2 and an amphitheater, the center hosts performances of dance, jazz, classical, comedy, Broadway and local theater, plus annual events like the Scottsdale Arts Festival and Culinary Festival.

Mesa Arts Center

1 East Main St., Mesa. 480-644-6500. www.mesaartscenter.com.

Three contemporary-industrial buildings totaling 212,775sq ft and 4 theaters with a total of 2,449 seats were built in 1992. The center showcases classical and popular music and dance. Local companies hosted here include Ballet Etudes, East Valley Children's Theatre, Metropolitan Youth Symphony, and Salt River Brass.

NIGHTLIFE

🍸 Arcadia Tavern

4801 E. Indian School Rd.,
Phoenix. 602-840-3950.
www.arcadiatavern.com.

Start with three dozen kinds of beer, add a chef-caliber menu of edibles like a half-pound cheese-stuffed burger or Granny Smith apple-brie-fig bruschetta, then top it off with any one of an assortment of high-end tequilas. The result is a fun, friendly spot to mix, mingle and watch sports within a watering hole whose setting is definitely urban-mod brick-n-butcher block.

🍸 Blue Hound Kitchen & Cocktails

In Hotel Palomar, 2 E. Jefferson St.,
Phoenix. 602-258-0231. www.
bluehoundkitchen.com.

The mixologists at this new (mid-2012) wood- and metal-trimmed gastropub don't just mix their drinks. They layer flavors and textures, working with more than 275 spirits, 70 wines, 20 craft beers, and 30 cocktail recipes that are constantly updated. "The Darkness," for example, is at once smoky, smooth and floral, blending Bols Genever Dutch gin, homemade lavender syrup, fresh lemon, mezcal, bitter amaro and egg white.

🍸 Four Peaks Brewing Company

1340 E. 8th St., Tempe. 480-303-9967. www.fourpeaks.com.

Revered by beer connoisseurs, this microbrewery opened in 1996 in the former Pacific Creamery brick building of 1890. The historic setting is the ideal backdrop for crafted on-site favorites like Four Peaks' Kiltlifter, 8th Street Ale, Hefeweizen, Hop Knot IPA, and seasonal batches like Pumpkin Porter and Arizona Peach Ale.

🍸 Handlebar J Restaurant & Saloon

7116 E. Becker Ln., Scottsdale. 480-948-0110. www.handlebarj.com.

Called "Wild Bill's" when it opened in 1960, this dark, barnlike hangout hosted acts like Waylon Jennings. Renamed in 1966 for the new owner's moustache, the venue now showcases the Herndon Brothers band. Cowboy music and two stepping still steal the show, antique cowboy hats hang from the rafters, and beer flows from the indoor-outdoor bar.

🍸 Harold's Cave Creek Corral

6895 E. Cave Creek Rd.,
Cave Creek. 480-488-1906.
www.haroldscorral.com.

Since the small original wood building opened in 1935, it's been home to resident lions and tigers living out back, Hollywood stars partying with dusty-boot cowboys inside, and some of the best live music to be found anywhere. The space has become huge over the years, now seating 600 indoors plus 200 on the patios, but somehow, a cozy mood still pervades for customers in search of a cold beer, a warm smile, or an invitation to dance.

EXCURSIONS

Apache Trail★★

Rte. 88 and US-60.

This 164mi loop includes a 78mi stretch of Route 88 between Apache Junction and Globe that crosses over the **Superstition Mountains**, skirts **Weaver's Needle Lookout** and passes three major lakes (Canyon, Apache and Roosevelt lakes) created by **Roosevelt Dam**. The 25mi from **Tortilla Flat**, a ghost town of six residents, to Roosevelt is a narrow, winding gravel road. En route, be sure to stop at the following two attractions:

Boyce Thompson Arboretum★
37615 Rte. 60, Superior. 520-689-2811. arboretum.ag.arizona.edu. Open summer months daily 6am–3pm, winter months daily 8am–5pm. Closed Dec 25. $9.
Mining magnate William Boyce Thompson turned this site that sits beneath Picketpost Mountain into a 300-acre public park in the 1920s. The 1.5mi main trail provides an overview; other trails take in a variety of vegetation that attracts a year-round colony of colorful birds. A hidden canyon, desert lake and interpretive center with two greenhouses are on-site.

Tonto National Monument★
Rte. 88, 4mi east of Roosevelt Dam. 928-467-2241. www.nps.gov/tont. Open year-round daily 8am–5pm. Closed Dec 25. $3. Reservations required.
This preserve holds the remains of 13C Salado Indian cliff dwellings. A .5mi trail climbs rather steeply to the 20-room Lower Dwelling

where the Salado lived. White cholla cacti, nicknamed "teddy bear," is plentiful along the way. The 3mi Upper Cliff Dwelling trail is open Nov–Apr.

Casa Grande Ruins National Monument★

1100 Ruins Dr., Rte. 87, Coolidge. 52mi southeast of Phoenix. Take Rte. 387 at I-10 Exit 185 and follow signs. 520-723-3172. www.nps.gov/cagr. Open year-round daily 9am–5pm. Closed Thanksgiving Day and Dec 25. $5.

Situated along the Gila River, this four-story, 60ft-long structure was among the last constructions of the 12C Hohokam people. Built of sand, clay and limestone mud, it became the first US archaeological preserve in 1892. South along the interstate lies **Picacho Peak State Park** *(I-10 Exit 219)*, a solitary 1,500ft-high landmark.

©National Park Service

Casa Grande Ruins National Monument

GREATER PHOENIX

Phoenix and the area around it are known as the Valley of the Sun, which has the hottest climate of any major metropolis in the US. The Phoenix metro area stretches across more than 2,000 square miles and takes in Scottsdale, Paradise Valley, Tempe, Mesa, Guadalupe, Chandler, Litchfield Park and other communities surrounding the relatively young urban center of Phoenix.

Thousands of years ago, this land of stark beauty was home to **Tohono O'odham** and **Hohokam** Indians, who built an elaborate **canal system** for irrigating fields of squash, beans and corn. In the 16C, Spaniards tramped through the mountains searching for gold, and though they found no riches, the *conquistadors* paved the way for priests and soldiers who established **missions** and walled forts called *presidios*. The US acquired most of modern-day Arizona in the aftermath of the **Mexican War** in 1848. The southern part of the state, from south of Phoenix to the current Mexican border became US territory as a result of the **Gadsden Purchase** in 1853. Soon after, folks came to mine or ranch. Today the sunshine and heat of the **Sonoran Desert** are the chief draws in one of the fastest-growing regions of the US.

CITIES

SCOTTSDALE
Founded as a farm village in 1888, Scottsdale *(480-421-1004; www. scottsdalecvb.com)* has blossomed into an upscale enclave for the well-to-do; today, it's full of resorts, golf courses and high-end shopping districts. Neighboring Phoenix to the east, it is edged by the **McDowell Mountains**, and hosts some 217,000-plus residents and more than 320 retail shops and 80 **art galleries**. The city is especially famed for its museums, art festivals and upscale **shopping centers** *(see Shopping below)*. **Downtown** Scottsdale is bounded roughly by Camelback Road., 2nd Street, 68th Avenue and Civic Center Boulevard *(480-947-6423; www.downtownscottsdale.com)*. For the last 30 years, galleries in this district *(Main St., Marshall Way and Fifth Ave.)* have scheduled new exhibits and artist appearances to coincide with **Scottsdale ArtWalk** *(Thu nights except Thanksgiving*

Bischoff's, Old Town Scottsdale

©Gwen Cannon/Michelin

Day, 7pm–9pm; free trolley shuttles).
Occupying the southeast corner of
Downtown, **Old Town★** *(Scottsdale
Rd., south of Indian School Rd.)*
is Scottsdale's historic district,
now a faux strip of the 19C West,
featuring wooden sidewalks,
hitching rails and rustic storefronts.
Many buildings now house
Southwestern-themed shops and
Native American art galleries. New
stores and condominiums have
been constructed along the canal.
Nearby **Scottsdale Mall** includes
the **Scottsdale Museum of
Contemporary Art** *(7374 E. 2nd St.;
480-874-4666; www.smoca.org)*,
the **Scottsdale Center for
the Performing Arts** and the
Scottsdale Historical Museum
*(7333 E. Scottsdale Mall; 480-945-
4499; www.scottsdalemuseum.com).*

TEMPE

*US-60 and Loop 202, 9mi east
of Phoenix. 866-914-1052.
www.tempetourism.com.*

Founded in 1871 on the **Salt
River**, this city of 164,000 is home
to **Arizona State University**.
The Tempe (tem-PEE) historical
district extends along Mill Avenue.
On the fringe of Papago Park, the
**Arizona Historical Society's
Museum at Papago Park**
*(1300 N. College Ave.; 480-929-9499;
www.arizonahistoricalsociety.org)*
focuses on Arizona's 20–21C
history. This college town has its
own **lake** *(80 W. Rio Salado Pkwy.;
480-350-8625; www.tempe.gov/lake;
open dawn-dusk)*, formed in the
bed of the Salt River; no swimming
is allowed, but strolls on the beach
and boating are permitted *(boat
rentals available).*

Arizona State University *(south
bank of Salt River east of Mill Ave.;
480-965-2100; www.asu.edu)* is
home to nearly 60,000 students.
Grady Gammage Auditorium★
*(Apache Blvd. and Mill Ave.; 480-
965-3434; www.asugammage.com)*,
is Frank Lloyd Wright's last major
nonresidential design (1959).
Antoine Predock's 1989 **J. Russell
and Bonita Nelson Fine Arts
Center★** *(10th St. and Mill Ave.)* is
a collision of boxes and triangles
that resembles a Hopi pueblo.

Guadalupe

*Avenida del Yaqui, south off
Baseline Rd. at I-10 Exit 155, Tempe.*

This settlement looks like a small
village in Mexico. It has a **farmers'
market** *(9210 W. Avenida del Yaqui;
480-730-1945; open Mon–Sat
10am–6pm, Sun 10am–5pm)*, a
Mexican bakery and a mercado.

MESA

*US-60 and Rte. 87, 15mi east
of Phoenix. 480-827-4700.
www.visitmesa.com.*

Founded by Mormon pioneers
in 1878, Mesa (pop. 447,000)
is the state's third-largest city.
Its downtown is charming. The
Mormon **Arizona Temple** *(525 E.
Main St.; 480-833-1211)* remains a
landmark. At huge **Falcon Field**
(Greenfield and McKellips Rds.),
the **Commemorative Air Force
Museum–Arizona Wing** *(2017
N. Greenfield Rd.; 480-924-1940;
www.azcaf.org)* showcases vintage
aircraft. In the spring, Mesa serves
as the **Cactus League** home
of Major League Baseball's
Chicago Cubs.

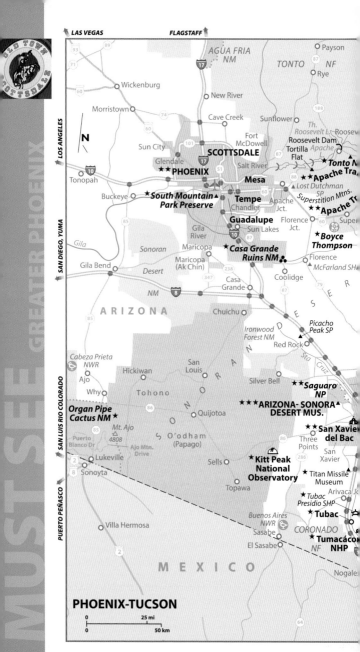

Show Low

Eagar

Carrizo

Alpine   Luna

Salt River
Canyon

Fort Apache

Hannagan
Meadow

San Carlos

APACHE-
SITGREAVES
NF

ARIZONA

Globe

San
Carlos

Glenwood

Peridot   San Carlos
L.

Mule
Creek

Coolidge
Dam   Bylas

Clifton

Winkelman

Dudleyville

CORONADO
NF

Pima   Gila

Solomon

San Manuel

Klondyke

Safford

Duncan

Roper
Lake SP

CORONADO
NF

PELONCILLO MTNS.

Mammoth

San Manuel

CORONADO
NF

Biosphere 2

Archaeology Southwest
Sabino Canyon ★★

TUCSON ★★

CORONADO NF

★★ Saguaro NP ▲

Pima Air & Space Mus. ★★

Colossal Cave ★

Vail

Bowie

Willcox

Fort Bowie
NHS ☆

Bonita
Canyon Drive

Willcox
Playa   Dos
Cabezas

Cochise

Faraway
Guest Ranch   Massai Pt.
△ 6870

NEW   MEXICO

Dragoon   ★ Amerind
Foundation
Mus.

★★ Chiricahua
NM

Kartchner
Caverns SP ▲

Benson

Sunizona

Rodeo

San Pedro &
Southwestern RR ★

San Pedro
Riparian NCA

SOUTHEAST

CORONADO
NF

Fort ☆
Huachuca

Fairbank

★ Tombstone ★★

ARIZONA ★

Tombstone
Courthouse SHP ★

Charleston

McNeal

Sierra Vista

Ramsey
Canyon ▲
Preserve

Bisbee ★★

CORONADO
NF

Slaughter
Ranch NHL

CORONADO
NF

Nogales

Montezuma Pass   6575

Naco

Douglas   San Bernardino
NWR

Agua Prieta

Miguel
Hidalgo

Cananea

HERMOSILLO

HISTORICAL SITES

Taliesin West★★

12621 Frank Lloyd Wright Blvd., via Taliesin Dr. off Cactus Rd., Scottsdale. 480-627-5340. www.franklloydwright.org. Guided tours (1hr-3hrs) Nov–Apr daily 9am–4pm every half hour, except Easter, Thanksgiving Day and Dec 25. $32.

Frank Lloyd Wright built this complex of low-lying buildings by gathering desert stone and sand from local washes. With its uneven rooflines, deeply shaded entrances and indigenous materials, Taliesin West remains a strong influence on design today. It served as his winter home from 1937 until his death in 1959, and is now the headquarters of the **Frank Lloyd Wright Foundation**.

Tours wind through the exquisitely landscaped **gardens★★**, with frequent stops on the terraces and walkways that connect the living quarters with Wright's private office. Also included are the Cabaret Theater, Seminar Theater and Music Pavilion. "Night Lights" tours *(Sept–May Fri evenings)* showcase Wright's fusion of light, architecture and landscape.

Cosanti

6433 Doubletree Ranch Rd., Paradise Valley. 928-632-6212. www.arcosanti.org/cosanti. Open for self-guided tours year-round Mon–Sat 9am–5pm, Sun 11am–5pm. Closed major holidays.

At this complex of buildings, Italian architect **Paolo Soleri** showcases his concept of "arcology," which he defines as the integration of architecture and ecology in new urban habitats. He began construction of his experimental structures in 1955. Today his home and sculpture studios are on-site. Bronze and ceramic bell-shaped **wind chimes**, made on the premises, grace the courtyards, and are for sale in the gift shop. At the foundry, visitors might see production in process.

A prototype, **Arcosanti**, is under construction an hour's drive north in Cordes Junction, off I-17 *(see NORTH-CENTRAL ARIZONA)*. The ultimate goal, according to the Arcosanti master plan, is to create a self-sustaining community of 5,000 that combines compact structures with large solar greenhouses.

Frank Lloyd Wright (1867-1959)

In the early 1930s, Wright and his wife Olgivanna founded an architectural school at their home in Wisconsin. Dubbed the "Taliesen Fellowship," the school mirrored Wright's passions, immersing students in the study of architecture, construction, gardening, farming and even music, art and dance. The brutal Wisconsin winters took their toll, however, and the Wrights and their students decided to spend the winter of 1934 in Arizona. Wright fell under the spell of the Sonoran Desert, and in 1937 he acquired a piece of land in the foothills of the McDowell Mountains. Here he built Taliesen West. For the rest of his life, he and his students migrated seasonally between Arizona and Wisconsin.

FOR KIDS

Arizona Museum of Natural History

53 N. Macdonald St., Mesa. 480-644-2230. www.azmnh.org. Open year-round Tue–Fri 10am-5pm; Sat 11am–5pm; Sun 1pm–5pm. Closed major holidays. $10; children $6.

This gem of a museum features Hohokam and pioneer history. Kids will especially like reconstructing a Woolly Mammoth using the museum's **3D Mammoth Puzzle**. The authentic territorial jails and the faithful re-creation of the **No Sweat Mine** are also favorites. And there isn't a child alive who doesn't like dinosaurs. The museum caters to this fascination with both a **Dinosaur Hall** featuring a variety of familiar dinosaur skeletons, and Dinosaur Mountain, where dinosaur replicas can be seen in settings that replicate what scientists believe were their native habitats.

Rawhide Western Town

5700 West North Loop Rd., Chandler. 480-502-5600. www.rawhide.com. Open year-round Wed–Fri 5pm–10pm (til 11pm Fri), Sat noon–11pm, Sun noon–10pm. Fees apply for rides.

Another area attraction that perpetuates the Old-West theme, this "town" re-creates an 1880s community with stagecoach rides, mock gunfights, and burro rides for children. Other activities include train rides, **panning for gold**, petting animals, and browsing in Western-style shops.

SHOPPING

SHOPPING MALLS

Arizona Center

400 E. Van Buren St. between N. 3rd and N. 5th Sts., Phoenix. 602-271-4000; www.arizonacenter.com. Open 24/7: shops generally open 11am and close 8pm–10pm.

Graced with fountains and sunken gardens, this complex anchors a corner in downtown Phoenix. Stores include **Flag World**, a supplier of flags and flag accessories; **Culture Fresh**, a contemporary men and women's clothing store; **Sports World**, a store selling logo-emblazoned apparel for professional and college sports teams. Places to eat include **1130 The Restaurant** as well as a Mexican and a Greek restaurant. The Starbucks coffeehouse is well patronized. There is also an AMC **movie theater** in the complex. Adjacent to the center, the **Herberger Theater's** Kax Stage *(southwest corner of Van Buren and 3rd St.; www.herbergertheater.org)* presents one-act plays during the lunch hour mid-week.

Kierland Commons

15205 N. Kierland Blvd., Scottsdale. 480-348-1577. www.kierlandcommons.com.

Scottsdale Fashion Square

©Gwen Cannon/Michelin

Scottsdale Fashion Square

7014 E Camelback Rd at N. Goldwater Blvd. 480-941-2140. www.fashionsquare.com.

This sprawling complex has more than 250 upscale shops, restaurants and department stores, with its own roving concierge. Scottsdale Fashion Square is justifiably known as one of the top shopping destinations in the Southwest. Armani, Ann Taylor, Banana Republic, Barney's New York, Brookstone, Bulgari and Cartier are just a few of the familiar big-name retailers. Dining options include Grand Lux Cafe (with a global menu) and Yard House (draft beer and American fare) as well as Mexican, sushi and steakhouse restaurants; Nordstrom and Neiman Marcus have cafes. Fortunately, there's plenty of on-site parking.

Opened in 2000, Kierland Commons covers a whopping 38 acres filled with 70 upscale retailers such as Anthropologie, Crate & Barrel, Smith & Hawken, Restoration Hardware and Tommy Bahama as well as local businesses. Tony restaurants include Bobby's (with a jazz lounge), North (Italian fare) and RA Sushi (Japanese fusion cuisine). Several high-end bars number among the mix. If you show your out-of-state driver's license at the Concierge Office *(between Tommy Bahama and Etch Salon),* you'll receive a free rewards book from the Scottsdale CVB *(480-348-1577).*

Shops at Hilton Village

6107-6149 N. Scottsdale Rd. 623-582-9599. www.hiltonvillage.com.

The Shops at Hilton Village center boasts 31stores ranging from Dolce Boutique (women's apparel) to Patrick James (men's apparel), and a wide variety of restaurants and coffee shops.

Legal Matters

When you buy Native American merchandise, it's best to purchase works that are produced by members of federally recognized tribes. Under the Indian Arts and Crafts Act, Native American art and crafts must be marketed honestly with regards to its heritage and producer's tribal affiliation. For more information, contact the Indian Arts and Crafts Board of the US Dept. of the Interior: 888-278-3253; www.iacb.doi.gov.

Summit at Scottsdale

Asher Hills Dr. and Scottsdale Rd., www.summitatscottsdale.com.

Home to the **Heard Museum North** *(480-488-9817; www.heard. org/north)*, Summit has a collection of fine restaurants, shops and salons. The shopping mall also meets practical needs with its tastefully appointed Target and Safeway stores.

SHOPPING DISTRICTS

Old Town Scottsdale

Scottsdale Rd. and Brown Ave., south of Indian School Rd.

Scottsdale's **historic district,** principally along Scottsdale Road and Brown Avenue, consists today of low-rise restaurants, bars and stores, many with a Southwest theme. Arizona souvenir shops, Western wear outfitters, Southwest furniture showrooms and Native American art galleries abound. Old Town's pink ice-cream parlor, the **Sugar Bowl** *(4005 N. Scottsdale Rd.; 480-946-0051; www.sugarbowlscottsdale.com)*, has been an institution since 1958. Old Town has its own **farmers' market** *(Oct–May Sat 8am–1pm; 623-848-1234; www. arizonafarmersmarkets.com)* held at the city parking facility *(Brown at 1st St., next to the Carriage House)*. Local growers showcase their produce and specialty foods with an emphasis on organic, pesticide-free products, including fresh cider and apples, flowers, natural pork and beef, free-range eggs, local cheeses, Amish friendship breads, jams and tamales.

Native American Works

Here's a sampling of Scottsdale's specialized galleries and shops.

Blue Rain Contemporary – *4164 N. Marshall Way. 480-874-8110. www.blueraingallery.com.* This gallery, which also has a location in Santa Fe, features pottery, sculpture, paintings and more—all created by a top-notch stable of contemporary artists.

Gilbert Ortega – *3925 N. Scottsdale Rd. and E. Main St., Old Town. 480-990-1808. www.gilbertortega.com.* This large gallery specializes in Native American art and jewelry. Silver and turquoise pieces abound.

The Heard Museum North – *32633 N. Scottsdale Rd. 480-488-9817. www.heard.org/north.* The museum shop here sells art, textiles, pottery, baskets and other American Indian works of art.

Old Territorial Indian Arts & Antiques – *7077 E. Main St. #7, 480-945-5432. www.oldterritorial shop.com.* A member of the Antique Tribal Art Dealers Association, this shop displays classic to contemporary pieces collected since 1969.

Scottsdale Trading Post – *7078 5th Ave. 480-945-1910. www.scottsdaletradingpost.com.* In business since 1958, this well-known gallery in the heart of the Scottsdale Arts District enjoys good relationships with Native American artists who work in a variety of media, including turquoise and silver jewelry, pottery and fetish carvings.

SHOPPING

109

SPAS

♨ Day Spas

Hand & Stone Massage and Facial Spa
15233 N. 87th St., Scottsdale. 480-991-5100. www.handand stone.com.

With multiple locations throughout the country, Hand & Stone is a spa that specializes in both massage and facials, with waxing thrown in, just for good measure. In the spa's signature treatment, a skilled massage therapist applies heated **river stones** to the back and other key areas, releasing tension and soothing away stress. Swedish, deep tissue and other forms of massage are available, plus men's and teen's facials.

Hawaiian Experience Spa
1949 W. Ray Rd. Chandler. 480-855-0145. www.hawaiian experiencespa.com.

The signature treatment here is the **Lomi Lomi**, a traditional massage perfected in Hawaii. Unlike standard massages, there is no bottom sheet in the Lomi Lomi. Instead, the customer lies directly on a massage table that is a covered with a thick film of essential oils. The therapist climbs onto the table at times, and at the end, there is a draping ceremony. Other exotic massages are offered, like the **Hot Sea Shell** massage. Any treatment here is best capped with a long stay in the steam room and a refreshing shower in a room that calls to mind a gentle Hawaiian waterfall. The spa has a second location in Chandler.

Kalologie 360 Spa
6107 N. Scottsdale Rd. 480-788-2360. www.kalologie.com.

Kalologie 360 offers customers a full range of treatments and services, including classic facials, as well as the signature **Kalologie Facial** that employs a pomegranate enzyme mask to exfoliate and stimulate cellular turnover. Other services such as peels, waxing and tanning are available. Swedish, Shiatsu, Sports, Deep Tissue and Pregnancy massages are on the spa menu.

Resort Spas

Aji Spa, Sheraton Wild Horse Pass Resort and Spa
5594 W. Wild Horse Pass Blvd. Chandler. 602.225.0100. www.wildhorsepassresort.com.

In the language of the Pima people, *aji* is translated as "sanctuary." And the feeling of sanctuary pervades this resort at the Gila River Indian Community. Owned jointly by the Pima and Maricopa tribes, the property celebrates their history and culture. Accordingly, the spa offers a menu based on traditional Native American therapies and practices. Developed by the resort's Pima and Maricopa cultural caretakers, it includes the Thoachta, or healing, treatment; the Pima Medicine Massage; the Vacht, or Indigenous Water Treatment; and the **Otham Kuklan**, or native herbs cleansing wrap. The spa experience is further enhanced by the inclusion of native design elements in the architecture and art throughout.

Centre for Well-Being, The Phoenician

6000 E. Camelback Rd. Scottsdale. 480-941-8200. www.thephoenician.com.

At this center the emphasis is on inner calm, self-revelation and harmony. The well-appointed facility offers massages, consultations and skin and body treatments, as well as a fitness studio, steam rooms, whirlpools and saunas. In addition to familiar massages, the center showcases "Signature Experiences": 50-110min treatments that include the **Desert Serenity Scrub**, Wrap and Massage, Papaya Quench Wrap, and Intraceuticals Infusion Facials. Instruction in meditation and tarot readings are also offered.

Four Seasons Resort Scottsdale at Troon North

10600 E. Crescent Moon Dr. 480-515-5700. www.fourseasons.com/ Scottsdale.

Luxury is the watchword at any Four Seasons resort, and the emphasis on understated luxury carries through to the resorts' spas and their services. The facility here offers all of the services one has come to expect from a first-class spa: massages, facial treatments, body treatments. Services run the gamut from hair styling to pedicures. But Four Seasons' signature treatments truly shine, namely the **Pinnacle Facial**, which pampers not only the face but the body with a gold-infused sugar scrub and shimmer oil; the Sedona Earth Clay Body Mask; and the Golfers' Massage that eases aches through the application of warm golf balls and stretching techniques.

Centre for Well-Being, The Phoenician

©The Phoenician

Willow Stream Spa, The Fairmont Scottsdale Princess

7575 E. Princess Dr. 480-585-4848. www.fairmont.com.

The design of this spa was inspired by a hidden oasis tucked away in the far reaches of the Grand Canyon. A waterfall, an atrium and a rooftop pool are designed around a theme of harmony, with air, water and fire brought together in perfect balance. In addition to a full slate of facials and massages, the spa is well known for its baths, such as a Thermal Mineral Bath, a Thalaso (detoxifying) Bath, and a calming Herbal Bath. Three signature experiences—**Havasupai Falls Rejuvenation**, Arizona Eucalyptus Salt Rub, and Desert Purification—are 60-120min sessions that have been specially designed to reinvigorate both mind and body.

SPAS

TUCSON★★

Home of Arizona's first university, Tucson is the state's second-largest city. Unlike Phoenix, which has conquered the desert with massive irrigation projects, Tucson embraces dry land. The city draws much of its water supply from the Central Arizona Project, a network of aquaducts, tunnels and pipelines built to transport water from the Colorado River to Tucson and the southern boundary of the San Xavier Indian Reservation, a distance of 336mi across the Sonoran Desert. With little or no agriculture, the city has come to consider green lawns a waste of time and water. Most residents focus on enjoying the plentiful sunshine and the high Sonoran Desert. Five mountain ranges surround this city that sprawls across 500sq mi. The Santa Catalina Mountains form the northern boundary of the metro area.

Tucson's **night skies** have inspired astronomers, professional and amateur, to set up telescopes. City regulations restrict outdoor lighting at night to preserve the starscape. Tucson's roots run deep, with people having inhabited the town site continuously for 12,000 years. The first stargazers, the **Hohokam**, left petroglyphs, ball courts and pit houses that may be seen in parks, canyons and excavations around the city. **Pima** and **Tohono O'odham** tribes later took up residence. The name "Tucson" was not applied until 1694, when Spanish missionaries

Fast Facts

Founded: August 20, 1775
Territorial capital: 1867-1877
Land area: 227 square miles
Metro population: 1 million
Record temperatures: hottest 117°F (June 26, 1990); coldest 6°F (Jan 7, 1913)
Average annual precipitation: 11.3 inches
Annual days of sunshine: 350

had trouble pronouncing *stjukshon*, an Indian word that means "spring at the foot of a black mountain." The city was founded in 1775 by Col. Hugo O'Conor, an Irish mercenary serving in the Spanish army. The walled **Presidio San Agustín del Tucson** was built under his direction; a reconstruction can be found in the **El Presidio Historic District**. Tucson became part of newly independent Mexico in 1821, then was transferred to the US with the **Gadsden Purchase** in 1853. It became capital of the Arizona Territory in 1867. The seat of government later moved north to Phoenix.

Downtown Tucson Buildings

©David Jewell/Metropolitan Tucson Convention & Tourism Bureau

Practical Information

When to Go

Tucson is about 1,000ft higher than Phoenix, so even though the seasons in the two cities are similar, Tucson enjoys marginally milder summers and cooler winters. **Summers** *(late May-late Sept)*, are oppressively hot, with average daytime temperatures Jun-Aug of 100°F. **Monsoon** thunderstorms, in late afternoon *(Jul-Aug)* provide some relief, but cause flash flooding in washes and riverbeds. Average overnight lows Jun-Aug are 73°F. Tucson is pleasant late Sept-late May. Average daily highs reach their low point in December (64.8°F) when overnight lows dip to 39°F. Overnight lows in the high 20s Dec and Jan are not uncommon.

Getting Around

◆ **From the Airport** – The main airport is **Tucson International Airport** (TIA) *(520-573-8100; www.flytucsonairport.com)*, located 20-30 min south of the city center at the end of South Tucson Blvd.

Bus: Sun Tran, the region's public transportation system, provides direct service to and from TIA via the No. 6 bus. From Ronstadt Transit Center downtown, passengers may make bus connections to all parts of the city. The trip between TIA and downtown takes 45-60min.

Taxi: Taxis can be found in front of the terminal on the lower roadway. Mileage to central Tucson is roughly 9 miles and rates include a $4.50 flag drop, $2.25/mi and $22/hr waiting time. **AAA Airport Cabs LLC** 520-299-8294; **Discount Cabs**

520-388-9000; **Flash Cab** 520-798-1111; **Yellow Cab** 520-624-6611.

Car Rental: Car-rental counters are at the rental-car parking garage adjacent to the main terminal.

◆ **By Public Transportation** – **Bus: Sun Tran** bus routes service all major destinations in the metropolitan area. For routes, fares and schedule, 520-792-9222; www.suntran.com.

Light Rail: A light rail system, Sun Link, is scheduled to go into operation in late 2013 or early 2014. The route (18 stops) runs roughly 4mi from the Univ. Medical Center, at the east end of the line, through UA campus, the 4th Ave. and downtown business districts, and terminates west of downtown on the west bank of the Santa Cruz River. www.tucsonstreetcar.com.

◆ **By Car** – Streets run north–south or east–west, except in the historic warehouse district, downtown. By convention, the north-south streets are designated as *avenues*. East-west streets are called *streets*. Major freeway I-10 runs from the northwestern suburbs to those in the southeast, skirting downtown's west side. I-19 runs south to the Mexican border after branching off from I-10 in the southern part of the city. **Rush hours** Mon–Fri are 7am–9am and 4:30pm–6pm.

Visitor Information

Tucson's visitor center is downtown in **La Placita complex** *(open year-round daily 9am–5pm, Sat–Sun 4pm; 520-624-1817. www.visittucson.org)*. Tucson is on Mountain Standard Time and does not observe Daylight Saving Time.

TUCSON

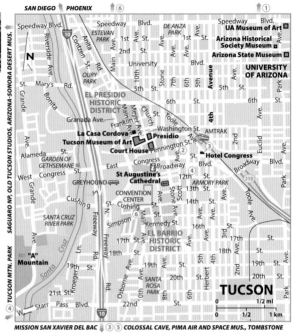

Map labels:

SAN DIEGO ♒ PHOENIX ⬆ ⑥   ⬆ ①

SAGUARO NP, OLD TUCSON STUDIOS, ARIZONA-SONORA DESERT MUS.

Speedway Blvd.   Speedway Blvd.   DE ANZA PARK   Speedway Blvd.

UA Museum of Art

Arizona Historical Society Museum

Arizona State Museum

UNIVERSITY OF ARIZONA

ESTEVAN PARK   1st St.   1st St.

University Blvd.

OURY PARK

EL PRESIDIO HISTORIC DISTRICT

Granada Ave.

La Casa Cordova
Tucson Museum of Art — Presidio
Court House   Pennington St.

AMTRAK

Hotel Congress

GARDEN OF GETHSEMANE

Congress   Broadway Blvd.

St Augustine's Cathedral

GREYHOUND

CONVENTION CENTER

ARMORY PARK

SANTA CRUZ RIVER PARK

EL BARRIO HISTORIC DISTRICT

"A" Mountain

SANTA ROSA PARK

TUCSON

0   1/2 mi
0   1/2   1 km

TUCSON MTN. PARK

CENTER FOR CREATIVE PHOTOGRAPHY, TUCSON BOTANICAL GARDENS

MISSION SAN XAVIER DEL BAC ⬆ ③ ⑤ COLOSSAL CAVE, PIMA AIR AND SPACE MUS., TOMBSTONE

HOTELS		RESTAURANTS	
Arizona Inn	①	Blue Willow	①
Canyon Ranch	②	Cafe Poca Cosa	②
Desert Diamond Casino Hotel	③	Cup Café in Hotel Congress	③
JW Marriott Starr Pass Resort	④	Downtown Kitchen & Cocktails	④
Loews Ventana Canyon	⑤	El Guero Canelo	⑤
Westward Look Resort	⑥	El Minuto	⑥

Tucson's **downtown** is condensed within a few square blocks east of I-10. Some old adobes and Spanish Colonial edifices remain. A walking tour takes in the 1896 **St. Augustine Cathedral** (192 S. Stone Ave.; 520-623-6351 www. augustinecathedral.org). At the original presidio site, Tucson's government complex includes the **Pima County Court House** (Church Ave. between Alameda and Pennington Sts.) with its tiled Spanish-style dome. El Presidio Historic District preserves 19C and early-20C houses and shops, including c.1850 **La Casa Cordova** (140 N Main Ave.).

Some 38,000 students attend the **University of Arizona★**, a top research institution. The 352-acre campus (between Euclid & Campbell Aves., 6th and Elm Sts; 520-621-2211; www.arizona.edu) lies 1mi northeast of downtown. About 800mi of **bike paths** make Tucson one of the best bicycling destinations in the US.

MUSEUMS

Arizona-Sonora Desert Museum★★★

*2021 N. Kinney Rd. 520-883-2702.
www.desertmuseum.org. Open
Mar–Sept daily 7:30am–5pm
(Jun–Aug Sat 10pm). Rest of the
year daily 8:30am–5pm. $14.50.*

A combination zoo, botanical park
and art gallery, this natural history
facility is devoted to the study and
appreciation of the surrounding
Sonoran Desert. It is best seen by
walking the 2mi of **trails** through
21 acres of the desert.
The museum is home to more
than 230 animal and 1,250 plant
species native to the Sonoran
Desert, the "world's lushest desert."
Ocelots and coatimundi prowl a
red-rock canyon, mountain lions
and Mexican wolves inhabit a
mountain woodland, bighorn
sheep climb rock ledges, and
javelina root among prickly
pears. Visitors meet the desert's
many raptors, such as Harris
hawks, in live demonstrations.
A purpose-built limestone cave
with stalagmites and stalactites
contains an **Earth Sciences★**

display. In the **Hummingbird
Aviary★★**, native hummingbirds
buzz by. **Life on the Rocks**
focuses on animals that inhabit
the rocky hillsides and mountain
peaks around Tucson, such as Gila
monsters, prairie dogs, rattlesnakes
and roadrunners. The new (2013)
Warden Aquarium illustrates the
vital role rivers like the Colorado
play in the Sonoran Desert.

Center for Creative Photography★★

*1030 N. Olive Rd. between E. 2nd
St. and Speedway Blvd. 520-621-
7968. www.creativephotography.
org. Open year-round Mon–Fri
9am–5pm. Sat–Sun 1pm–4pm.
Closed major holidays.*

Founded in 1975 by University of
Arizona President John Schaefer
and Ansel Adams, the center
celebrates photography as an
art form, and retains the archives
of more than 60 photographers,
including Ansel Adams, Edward
Weston, Garry Winogrand and
Harry Callahan. Although the
works of Adams and other

Ferruginous Hawk, Arizona-Sonora Desert Museum

©Phil Coleman/Arizona-Sonora Desert Museum

photographers represented in the CCP archives are often featured, the center's exhibits draw from the work of other contemporary photographers. **Photo Friday**, an opportunity to view select prints from the collection, is offered the first Friday of the month (*11:30am–3:30pm*) in the Volkerding Room (*2nd floor*).

Arizona Historical Society Museum Tucson★

949 E. 2nd St., across Park Ave. from UA campus. 520-628-5774. www.arizonahistoricalsociety.org. Open year-round Mon–Sat 10am–4pm. $5.

Exhibits include a **stagecoach** that was used on the Tombstone-Fairbank route, military gear and uniforms, and Spanish **silverwork.** Personal items used by Wyatt Earp and Geronimo are also on display.

Arizona State Museum★

On University of Arizona campus, 1013 E. University Blvd. at Park Ave. 520-621-6302. www.statemuseum. arizona.edu. Open year-round Mon–Sat 10am–5pm. Closed major and state holidays. $5.

This anthropology museum specializes in the cultures of the Southwest and Mexico. In the north building, the **Paths of Life★★** exhibit interprets origins, history and modern lifestyles of 10 desert cultures. **The Pottery Project** exhibit features some of the museum's more than 20,000 whole vessels, the largest and most comprehensive collection of Southwest American Indian pottery in the world.

Tucson Museum of Art and Historic Block★

140 N. Main Ave. 520-624-2333. www.tucsonmuseumofart.org. Open year-round Wed–Sat 10am–5pm (Thu til 8pm), Sun noon–5pm. Closed Thanksgiving Day and Dec 25. $10.

This contemporary museum showcases avant-garde art and photography, plus fine 19–20C works by renowned American and international artists including Chuck Close, Marsden Hartley, Jasper Johns, and Max Weber. The museum also boasts a **sculpture garden** and a gallery of Western art. The museum's **Historic Block** is located at the northwest corner of what was once the Presidio of San Augustin del Tucson. The block consists of five houses that surround the museum and its sculpture garden. These properties date from the mid-1850s to 1907.

UA Museum of Art★

On University of Arizona campus, 1031 N. Olive Rd.; between E. 2nd St. and Speedway Blvd. 520-621-7567. artmuseum.arizona.edu. Open year-round Tue–Fri 9am–5pm, Sat–Sun noon–4pm. Closed major and university holidays. $5.

Paintings by Rembrandt, Picasso and Rothko, and Jacques Lipchitz sculptures highlight a 5,000-piece collection dating from the 14C to contemporary times. Also displayed is the 26-panel *Retablo de la Cathedral de la Ciudad Rodrigo* by 15C Spanish painters Fernando Gallego and Maestro Bartolomé, perhaps the finest late-Gothic Spanish painting in the US.

HISTORICAL SITES

Mission San Xavier del Bac★★

1950 W. San Xavier Rd., south of downtown, off I-19. 520-294-2624. www.sanxaviermission.org. Open year-round daily 7am–5pm.

San Xavier del Bac was founded in 1692 by Father Eusebio Kino, though the Catholic mission wasn't finished until 1797. With bricks, stone and limestone mortar, Tohono O'odham Indians created an exquisite white-domed building of Mexican Renaissance, Moorish and Byzantine styles.

The walls and ceilings of the **sanctuary**, entered through heavy mesquite-wood doors, are painted in historical **frescoes**. Throughout are statues and carvings. Small handmade objects with ribbons, **milagros**, are left by people seeking a miracle or giving thanks. Although it still serves parishioners as a place of worship, San Xavier has a small **museum** devoted to the mission and Father Kino. A small hill east of the church affords **views** of the mission and the surrounding desert. Across from the church, a **plaza** holds shops selling Native American arts and crafts.

Presidio San Agustín del Tucson★

Church and Washington Sts. 520-837-8119. www.tucson presidiotrust.org. Open Jun–Sept Thu–Sun 10am–3pm. Rest of the year daily 10am–4pm.

A recent (2007) reconstruction of the **1775 Presidio** recalls life at the fort. Established by Hugo O'Conor, the 11-acre presidio was originally encircled by a wooden palisade. Less than 10 years later, an adobe wall 8ft-12ft tall was erected after the fort was attacked by the Apache. Occupied until 1856, the fort was demolished thereafter, and the remaining wall torn down in 1918.

Today visitors can see the reconstructed 10ft tall walls and 20ft adobe tower. Be sure to visit the **museum** housed inside a refurbished adobe structure (*Meyer St.*), and see the **mural wall** (*south side*) that provides a window onto the rest of the fort.

Archaeology Southwest

300 N. Ash Alley. 520-882-6946. www.archaeologysouthwest.org. Check website for time and place.

Archaeologists host and participate in events in which they discuss various aspects of their research into the cultural history of the Southwest. These gatherings are held in various locations throughout the Southwest, including Tucson, Phoenix, Colorado and New Mexico *(a full schedule is available on the website)*. The organization also hosts an informal **Archaeology Cafe** the second Tuesday of every month *(6pm)* at the Casa Vicente restaurant in Tucson *(375 S. Stone Ave.; 520- 884-5253)*. Researchers lead lively discussions on an array of research topics. These events are free and open to the public.

HISTORICAL SITES

PARKS AND GARDENS

Saguaro National Park★★

520-733-5100. www.nps.gov/sagu. Open daily dawn–dusk. $10/ vehicle or $5/person (on foot or bicycle).

The giant saguaro, iconic symbol of the Southwest, grows only in the Sonoran Desert of Arizona and northern Mexico. This park protects thriving stands of the cacti, which can grow to 50ft in height, 8 tons in weight and 200 years in age. Saguaros anchor diverse communities of animals and smaller plants.

The park has two units. In the 37sq mi **Tucson Mountain District** *(2700 N. Kinney Rd.; 520-733-5158)*, saguaros are thicker and younger. Beginning from the Red Hills Visitor Center, 1mi north of the Desert Museum, trails and the **Bajada Loop Drive** *(9mi)* offer fine views of cacti climbing mountain slopes. Starting 3.5mi north of the visitor center, the **Valley View Overlook Trail** *(.8mi)* offers fine views of Avra Valley and Picacho Peak.

The 103sq mi eastern unit of the national park, the **Rincon**

Mountain District *(3693 S. Old Spanish Trail; 520-733-5153)*, lies on the east side of Tucson, 15mi from downtown.

The **Cactus Forest Drive** *(8mi)* loops from the visitor center through a saguaro forest; 128mi of hiking and horse **trails** climb over 7,000ft ridges into a woodland shared by scrub oak and ponderosa pine.

Colossal Cave Mountain Park★

16721 E. Old Spanish Trail, 6mi north of I-10 Exit 279, Vail, 25mi southeast of Tucson. 520-647-7275. www.colossalcave.com. Open mid-Mar–mid-Sept daily 8am–5pm. Rest of the year daily 9am–5pm. $5/vehicle (park access). $13 (tour).

Tours *(45-60min)* of this large, dry cave follow a half-mile route planned by the Civilian Conservation Corps in the mid-1930s. The cave serves as the home or way station to almost half the **bat species** found in Arizona.

Saguaro National Park

©National Park Service

MUST DO TUCSON

The Giant Saguaro

The giant saguaro (se-WAR-oh) is found only in the highly specialized **Sonoran Desert** climate. The largest species of cactus in the US grows slowly: after three years, a young saguaro is barely half an inch high. It will be 50 years old before it flowers, and 75 years of age before it sprouts its first arm. An individual saguaro produces some 40 million seeds, but generally only one develops into a mature plant. For germination, heavy summer rains must fall; of those that sprout, only one percent survive. It's illegal to damage saguaros or remove them from the desert, living or dead, without a permit. But poaching has long been a problem. Investigators for the Arizona Department of Agriculture, sometimes called "Cactus Cops," patrol the desert in search of violators. The ultimate revenge was exacted years ago on a Phoenix man who began blasting a saguaro with a 16-gauge shotgun. A spiny 4ft arm fell off the cactus, crushing the vandal.

Tucson Botanical Gardens★

2150 N. Alvernon Way, south of Grant Rd. 520-326-9686. www.tucsonbotanical.org. Open year-round daily 8:30am–4:30pm. Closed major holidays. $13 Oct–Apr, $8 May–Sept.

This 5.5-acre urban oasis hosts gardens containing a variety of cacti, wildflowers and Native American crops. A **xeriscape garden** demonstrates landscaping in an arid climate. Since the plants are labeled, this garden is a great place to orient yourself to desert flora. It's hard to believe just how many types of cactus there are.

Tucson Mountain Park

Gates Pass and Kinney Rds. www.pima.gov/nrpr/parks. Open year-round daily dawn–dusk.

Here, some 27sq mi of mountain and mesa lands encompass one of the world's most magnificent saguaro forests. Much of west Tucson is embraced within this parkland. The **views** of both the city and the surrounding desert from **Gates Pass** are spectacular.

©Randy Larson

Tucson Botanical Gardens

THE GREAT OUTDOORS

Sabino Canyon★★

5900 N. Sabino Canyon Rd.
at Sunrise Dr. 520-749-1900.
www.sabinocanyon.org. Open
year-round daily 9am–4:30pm.

Part of the Coronado National
Forest, Sabino Canyon lies in the
foothills of the **Santa Catalina
Mountains**. Once visited by
mammoths in prehistoric times
and much later, soldiers, who
rode from Fort Lowell to swim,
the canyon was "civilized" in the
1930s. Flash floods here in 2005
demonstrated the power of
summer thunderstorms. Resident
wildlife include javelina, white-
tailed deer, snakes, road runners
and tarantulas. The canyon is
closed to automobile traffic, with
access limited to hikers, bicyclists,
and those who take advantage
of the trams operated by **Sabino
Canyon Tours** *(520-749-2861;
ww.sabinocanyon.com)*. The
trams navigate both the **Sabino
Canyon Trail** in summer *(Mon–Fri*

9am–4pm, Sat–Sun til 4:30pm; $8)
and winter *(daily 9am–4:30pm; $8)*
and the **Bear Canyon Trail** *(daily
9am–4:30pm, on the hour; $3)*.
Tours to see canyon flora and
fauna at night are available in
certain months.

"A" Mountain

Sentinel Peak Rd., off Congress St.

Overlooking downtown, this
"hill" is nicknamed for a big letter
"A" whitewashed on the side of
Sentinel Peak in 1915 by fans of
the university football team. It's
a popular hiking destination;
views★★ are excellent from atop
the peak.

Tumamoc Hill

*West on Congress St., across
the Santa Cruz River 2mi from
downtown. Closed to the public
weekdays 7:30am–5:30pm.
No dogs or smoking allowed.*

Hiking this approximately 700ft
high hill is a popular pastime
of area residents. Because it is a
university **field research site**,
hours of visitation are restricted. A
challenging climb, the paved path
rises rather steeply, winding up
the hill and revealing magnificent
views★★ of downtown Tucson
and points beyond. At the midway
point, the scattered historic stone
buildings encountered are part
of the **Desert Laboratory** *(not
open to the public)*. En route, deer,
javelina and rattlesnakes might be
seen. Saguaro, cholla and prickly
pear cacti, wildflowers and other
plants line the trail. *Hikers are
cautioned to stay on the path.*

"A" Mountain

©Joyce Holly/Michelin

FOR KIDS

Pima Air and Space Museum★★

6000 E. Valencia Rd. at I-10 Exit 267. 520-574-0462. www.pimaair. org. Open year-round daily 9am–5pm. $13.75, children $8, ages 6 years and under free.

This outdoor-indoor museum boasts a full replica of the Wright Brothers' **1903 Flyer**. The SR-71 Blackbird on view is capable of speeds of more than 2,000mph. Visitors see some 275 military, private and commercial aircraft and spacecraft, including the **Air Force One** used by President John Kennedy.

Tours visit the **Aerospace Maintenance and Regeneration Center** on the Davis-Monthan Air Force Base, where retired aircraft are stored. The **Challenger Learning Center** enrolls kids in space "missions."

Pima operates the **Titan Missile Museum**★ (*1580 W. Duval Mine Rd., Sahuarita, at I-19 Exit 69, 25mi south of Tucson; 520-625-7736; www. titanmissilemuseum.org; open daily 8:45am–5pm; $8.50, children $5, ages 6 and under free*), a chilling reminder of the Cold War. For two decades, the US kept 54 nuclear warhead missiles ready to be launched at a moment's notice from various sites. All except this site were dismantled in the 1980s.

Old Tucson Studios★

201 S. Kinney Rd. 520-883-0100. www.oldtucson.com. Open year-round Oct–May Fri–Sun 10am–4pm. $16.95, children (ages 4-11) $10.95.

Hollywood in the desert, this former 1880s **Western town** has been the location for more than 350 movies and TV shows since it was built in 1939 by Columbia Pictures as the set for *Arizona*, starring William Holden. John Wayne *(Rio Lobo, 1966; McClintock, 1962)* made several films here; Clint Eastwood *(The Outlaw Josey Wales, 1976)* and Paul Newman *(Hombre, 1966)* were among other stars who filmed here.

The dusty frontier town was turned into an entertainment park in 1959, but has continued to operate as a film set. Visitors can saunter by jails, saloons and dance halls. **Town Hall** is a museum of film history. There are also stunt shows, stagecoach rides, gunfights, theaters, and a thrilling **Iron Door Mine Ride**.

Flandrau Science Center and Planetarium

On University of Arizona campus, 1601 E. University Blvd. at Cherry Ave. 520-621-4515. www.flandrau.org. Open year-round Mon–Fri 10am–3pm (Thu–Fri also 6pm–9pm), Sat 10am–9pm, Sun 1pm–4pm. $7.50, children $5, 4 and under free.

Interactive exhibits deal with mirrors, vacuums, holograms, kinetics and other basic physics at this science center. Permanent exhibits highlight the planet **Mars** with a large-scale model of its surface, as well as a display titled **Colliding Astroids**. Planetarium shows are regularly scheduled, and the **observatory** offers stargazing through a 16in telescope.

FOR KIDS

121

SHOPPING

SHOPPING HUBS

La Encantada

2905 E. Skyline Dr., at Campbell Ave.
520-615-2561. www.laencanta
dashoppingcenter.com.

This two-level, open-air shopping
center boasts upscale retailers
such as Anthropologie, Brooks
Brothers, Coach, Cole Haan,
J. Crew, Louis Vuitton, Pottery Barn,
St. John, Talbots, Tiffany & Co. and
Tommy Bahama. Outdoor plazas, a
number of restaurants, and on-site
parking are other pluses.

The Lost Barrio

South Park Ave., south of
Broadway. www.lostbarrio
tucson.com.

This row of low-lying brick
buildings on one side of the street
and vibrantly painted adobe
structures on the other stretches
for about three blocks. Former
brick warehouses have been
transformed into handsome—

some cavernous—retail spaces
selling antique furniture, arts and
crafts, and myriad gift items.

MAST *(www.ilovemast.com)* is
a roomy, light-filled atelier where
handmade creations are displayed.
Three local artists collaborate to
design lamps and shades, handmade greeting cards, furniture,
moccasins, leather belts and
other items. **Eclectic Flea** holds
a hodgepodge of **vintage
clothing**, and household pieces.
Petroglyphs, **Eastern Living** and
Colonial Frontiers are among the
other stores where just browsing
is a treat. Have breakfast or lunch
at **Tooley's Cafe** *(www.tooleys
cafe.com)* in its shady patio.

Old Town Artisans

201 N. Court Ave. 520-623-6024.
www.oldtownartisans.com.

This restored 1850s adobe in **El
Presidio** has shops selling Latin
American folk art and Native
American tribal art. A Spanish-style
courtyard is graced with regional

Shops along Tucson's 4th Avenue

©Joyce Holly/Michelin

plants, and a cantina serves food and drinks. Evenings *(Wed–Fri)* and Sunday afternoons, musicians perform in the open-air courtyard.

4th Avenue

University Blvd. south to 9th St. and the 4th Ave. Underpass. www.fourthavenue.org.

As the major thoroughfare connecting the university and its surrounding neighborhoods to downtown, this avenue serves as the city's melting pot. Shops and restaurants sit side-by-side in an eclectic mix, reflecting what is left of Tucson's hippie culture along with thriving cowpunk, Goth and information-age sensibilities. On warm weekend evenings when the sidewalks fill up with locals, especially college students, a carnival-like atmosphere prevails. Twice a year, the **4th Avenue Street Fair** *(late Mar and early Dec)* brings vendors together for a weekend-long celebration of arts, crafts and al fresco dining. Here's a sampling of 4th Avenue retailers:

Creative Ventures Craft Mall
522 N. 4th Ave. 520-792-3954. www.Tucson-Creative-Ventures.com.
An avenue landmark, this large (4,000sq ft) craft mall features a mix of **souvenirs**, jewelry, crafts, and Southwestern food items. In the same location for 20 years, Ventures is a favorite with locals, students and tourists alike.

Hippie Gypsy
351 N. 4th Ave. 520-624-0667.
So old-school, it doesn't even have a website, Hippie Gypsy is the quintessential head shop, and one of the last outposts of Tucson's

countercultural heyday. The place to go to stock up on posters, T-shirts, incense and warm feelings of déjà vu for aging Baby Boomers.

How Sweet It Was
419 N. 4th Ave. 520-623-9854. www.howsweetitwas.com.
Open since 1974, the venerable avenue landmark stocks thousands of items ranging from formal- and daywear to wedding gowns and tuxedos. The focus is clothing and accessories that date from 1870 to 1970, including vintage **cowboy boots**, but the shop also features a large selection of vintage linens, quilts and tablecloths.

Olytata
400 N. 4th Ave. 520-622-8932.
Drawing on cultural influences from both sides of the border, Olytata's embodies the spirit of both 4th Avenue and downtown Tucson's arts scene. The shop carries a mix of jewelry, souvenirs, and items that carry images of Catholic saints. An extensive selection of skeleton statues reflects the enduring popularity of the la Dia de los Muertos holiday.

Pop-Cycle Shop
422 N. 4th Ave. 520-622-3297. www.popcycleshop.com.
Repurposed is this shop's middle name. The retail store is a real **recycle** shop with many items made from license plates, old wood, cans and bottles, and funky art. Notebooks created from vinyl records, belts from vehicle seatbelts, apparel, accessories, decorations, pottery, furniture, local greeting cards—you name it.

SHOPPING

123

INDIVIDUAL STORES

Antigone Books

411 N. 4th Ave. 520-792-3715.
www.antigonebooks.com.

Antigone recalls the days when bookstores were quiet gathering places where people could meet, share ideas, or begin personal journeys on the wings of some newly discovered author's imagination. The staff knows books and is not shy when it comes to making recommendations. There are books for every age group, and greeting cards and gift items as well. The bookstore also hosts readings by touring authors.

Bon

3022 E. Broadway. 520-795-2272.
www.bon-boutique.com.

This cozy, fascinating shop is run by a mother-daughter team who welcomes patrons as if in their own home. A variety of merchandise, attractively displayed, includes items for home and garden as well as adult and children's fashions. The clothes are made mostly by US companies, and home items are crafted by locals. Linens found in France, rugs from Bolivia and baby items, in particular, are irresistible.

Bookmans

1930 E. Grant Rd. 520-325-5767
and 6230 E. Speedway Blvd. 520-
748-9555. www.bookmans.com.

Another enduring Tucson institution, this "entertainment exchange" was once known primarily as a big used bookstore. If you were looking for an obscure or out-of-print title, or if you just wanted a good cheap read, Bookmans was the place to go. As tastes and technologies have changed over the last 30 years, so has this retailer. Today, Bookmans offers used records, CDs, DVDs, magazines, games, gaming systems, musical instruments and more. Every trip is an adventure, since, as Heraclitus might say, you never step into the same Bookmans twice. The stock is constantly changing, with an inventory largely determined by what customers brought in to exchange for cash or credit the day before. That's frustrating if you're searching for a particular book or movie, but the thrill of discovering some altogether unexpected treasure is ample compensation. Both stores have seating and out-of-the-way nooks where patrons can read, meditate or even nap before moving on to find the next gem.

Desert Bloom

27 N. Stone Ave. 520-792-9882.

This modest downtown shop attracts passersby (namely ladies) with its enticing window display of handbags, jewelry and women's hats, as well as a home-decor bauble or two. Somewhat pricey women's clothing and accessories are carefully selected, and frequently refreshed, by the owner, who gives each customer personal attention and feedback. There's usually a rack of reduced apparel in the back room. And for holidays and certain city events, a few special souvenirs (like a Day of the Dead tree ornament) are displayed and for sale.

PERFORMING ARTS

Fox Tucson Theater

17 W. Congress St. 520-547-3040.
www.foxtucsontheatre.org.

A landmark since 1929, this
majestic theater remains the
grand dame of Tucson arts and
entertainment. As the property
continues to undergo restoration
of its **Southwestern Art Deco**
features, it hosts performances
of anything from internationally
celebrated banjo talent and
Elvis-theme theater, to classic and
independent movie screenings
and an annual India festival.

Rialto Theatre

318 E. Congress St. 520-740-1000.
www.rialtotheatre.com.

The intimate concert hall (1920)
maintains its historic charm,
down to the stacked, movie-style
marquee out front, but updated
with a state-of-the-art sound
system. Entertainment in the Art
Nouveau space focuses on music

from acoustical, hip-hop and rock
to world and flamenco, as well as
stand-up comedy acts and family
friendly holiday sing-alongs.

Tucson Music Hall

260 S. Church Ave. 520-791-4101.
www.tucsonaz.gov/tcc.

This 2,289 seat hall in the **Tucson
Convention Center** hosts a
large roster of talent, including
the Tucson Symphony Orchestra,
Tucson Regional Ballet and Arizona
Opera. Traveling shows performing
at the Expressionist-Modern
designed structure include Blue
Man Group and Wicked.

Club Congress

In Hotel Congress, 311 E.
Congress St. 520-622-8848.
www.hotelcongress.com.

The dance club in the landmark
Hotel Congress (1919) is hardly
considered a proper performing
arts venue, yet garage-chamber
classical music is presented
here. The club mainly features
alternative music, acoustic guitar
and jazz, sounds so beloved
that the spot has its own Club
Congress DeliRadio station.

©Joyce Holly/Michelin

Fox Tucson Theater

Tucson's Big Catch

A fire in **Hotel Congress** in
1934 led to the capture of
fugitive **John Dillinger** and
his gang. Extradited to the
Midwest, Dillinger later
escaped, only to die in a hail
of bullets in Chicago that
same year.

EXCURSIONS

Kitt Peak National Observatory★

Rte. 86, Tohono O'odham Reservation, 56mi southwest of Tucson. 520-318-8732. www.noao. edu/kpno. Open year-round daily 9am–3:45pm. $9.75.

Funded by the National Science Foundation, this observatory atop 6,875ft **Kitt Peak** houses the world's largest collection of optical telescopes. Tours (*1hr*) canvass an array of observatories up to 18 stories tall. The nightly viewing program offers visitors glimpses of planets and distant galaxies through 16in and 20in telescopes.

Organ Pipe Cactus National Monument★

Rte. 85, 140mi west of Tucson via Rte. 86. 520-387-6849. www.nps. gov/orpi. Check website for visitor center hours. $4, $8/vehicle.

This 516sq mi preserve on the Mexican border is the only place

in the US to see wild organ pipe cacti, cousins of the saguaro. In spring and summer, their lavender-white, night-blooming flowers open. Gravel-surfaced **Ajo Mountain Drive** (*21mi*) winds along the foothills of the 4,800ft Ajo Range. **Puerto Blanco Drive** (*5mi*) accesses the Pinkley Peak Picnic Area.

Biosphere 2

32540 S. Biosphere Rd., near Oracle, 40mi north of Tucson. 520-838-6200. www.b2science.org. Open year-round daily 9am–4pm for guided tours. $20.

The spaceship-like facility in which eight researchers lived from 1991 to 1993 is managed by the University of Arizona. Guided tours lead visitors through parts of the self-sustaining laboratory.

Mount Lemmon

Catalina Hwy., off Tanque Verde Rd., 32mi northeast of Tucson. 520-749-8700. www.fs.usda.gov/recarea/ coronado/recreation.

With an elevation of 9,157ft, Mount Lemmon boasts temperatures 20-30 degrees cooler than in the valley below. The drive to the summit is a series of switchbacks through a rapid succession of habitats, ranging from the scrub desert of the valley floor to lush pine forests. **Trails** offer sweeping **views★★** of the Tucson area. In winter, temperatures drop below freezing, and snows at the higher elevations can create hazardous driving conditions.

Organ Pipe Cactus National Monument

©National Park Service

SOUTHEAST ARIZONA★

Straddling I-19 south of Tucson and stretching eastward to the New Mexico border, below I-10, Southeast Arizona is marked with higher elevations and cooler temperatures than Tucson. A landscape that reverberates with familiar echoes of Old West history, the lower part of the state is full of intriguing places, many informed by the legendary personalities of the past. Here the Apache Indians—led by Cochise and later, Geronimo—battled the US Cavalry to a standstill. Here Wyatt Earp and Doc Holliday got into a disagreement with the Clanton Gang at the O.K. Corral. The most prosperous early communities in the Arizona Territory were in the far southeast. The copper town of Bisbee had opera, money and Victorian architecture. Tombstone's silver mine was fabulously productive, its citizens wealthy, its restaurants "the best between New Orleans and San Francisco." Today the rugged mountains, desert vistas and superb birding spots of this former frontier bordering Mexico complement its colorful past with some of the most impressive scenery in the Southwest.

Europeans first entered what is now Southern Arizona in 1540, when Francisco Vasquez de Coronado, searching for the legendary **Seven Cities of Gold**, led his expedition north from present-day Mexico into the valley of the **San Pedro River**. Coronado's expedition ended in failure, and the path he blazed through the San Pedro Valley—which runs north and south midway between present-day **Bisbee** and Sierra Vista—was largely ignored by European settlers until the mid-1800s. Then, in 1877, Jack Dunn discovered **copper** in the Mule Mountains. That discovery led to the founding of Bisbee, the "Queen of the Copper Camps." The same year that Dunn found copper in the Mules, Ed Schieffelin went into the hills east of the San Pedro River, looking for precious metals. He found **silver**, and a settlement with the unlikely name of **Tombstone** became the center of the silver-mining activity.

Settlers poured into the region to work the mines and to build the **Southern Pacific Railroad**, which still runs roughly parallel to Interstate 10. These developments led to a growing demand for food, which in turn attracted the attention of cattlemen who moved in to graze cattle on the area's abundant open range. With their arrival, **cowboy culture** came to Southern Arizona. The silver mines around Tombstone soon played themselves out, but Bisbee's mines produced high-grade copper ore up until the mid-1970s when Phelps Dodge shut down its mining operations there.

Touring Tip

For more information about Southeast Arizona, call 520-432-9215 or go online to www.explorecochise.com. Tucson's official tourism bureau can provide information on the area too: 520-624-1817 or www.visittucson.org.

CITIES

TUBAC

I-19 Exit 34, 45mi south of Tucson. 520-398-2704. www.tubacaz.com.

Evidence suggests that Tubac has been inhabited for some 11,000 years. The earliest settlers were likely the "Elephant Hunters," or **Paleo Indians**, who lived side-by-side with the great Mammoths that roamed the forests of prehistoric Arizona. The Elephant Hunters were followed by the **Hohokam** people, who lived in Arizona from roughly 300-1500 AD. After the Hohokam vanished—a disappearance that remains a mystery to this day—the **Pima** and **O'odham** people settled in the area. It was the Pima and O'odham who greeted the legendary Jesuit priest and missionary Eusebio Francisco Kino as he made his way up the Santa Cruz River valley in 1691. Kino died in 1711, but by 1738 his followers had established a mission ranch and farm on the site. And in 1752, the Spanish established a fort (the Presidio of San Ignacio de Tubac) there, on the banks of the Santa Cruz. The community has endured through a succession of governments—Spanish, Mexican and finally, American—and survives today as a thriving artists' colony and charming way station on the road from Tucson to Mexico.

Tubac Presidio State Historic Park★

Tubac Rd. at Burreul St. 520-398-2252. www.tubacpresidiopark.com. Open year-round daily 9am–5pm. $4.

Shopping in Tubac

This town is a popular mecca for shoppers. A variety of crafted products entice browsers and buyers such as hand-painted tiles, handmade pottery, furniture carved of wood, and textiles. Mexican wares are also for sale here. October to May is the busy season, when shops are open daily (but Monday closures are common). In the heat of the summer, many shops are closed. Housed in a handsome Spanish Colonial building, the newly expanded **Tubac Center of the Arts** *(9 Plaza Rd.; 520-398-2371; www.tubacarts.org)* sells jewelry, paintings, ceramic pieces and other interesting wares—many made by area artists—in its gift shop.

This state park recounts the 260-year history of the presidio (fortress). The presidio was built in 1752 in response to an uprising led by the Pima warrior Luis. Although the uprising was initially successful, Spanish forces defeated Luis and his followers in the Santa Catalina Mountains north of present-day Tucson. The Pima people eventually accepted the presence of the Spanish, but the Apaches, who ranged freely through the mountains and valleys east of Tubac, posed an ongoing threat to both the agrarian Pimas and the Spanish colonists. In the face of the Apache threat, the presidio at Tubac remained an important **military outpost** while becoming the focal point of a

Reenactment of O.K. Corral Gunfight

©Rick Machle/Metropolitan Tucson Convention & Tourism Bureau

growing community. Today, the presidio serves as a state historic park where visitors can explore an **underground archaeology exhibit** as well as a **museum** that gives a broad overview of human history in the Santa Cruz valley. Also featured is a **printing press** that was used to print Arizona's first newspaper in 1859, and an art gallery that features works by noted Western artist William Ahrendt. Numerous events throughout the year celebrate the area's crafts and agricultural history.

TOMBSTONE★★

US-80 between Benson and Bisbee, 67mi southeast of Tucson via I-10 Exit 303. 520-457-3929. www.tombstone.org.

"The Town Too Tough to Die" transports visitors back to the year 1881, when Marshal **Wyatt Earp**, his brothers and **Doc Holliday** vanquished the cattle-rustling **Clanton Gang** in the legendary "Gunfight at the O.K. Corral." Buildings still stand from the halcyon mining years of

1877-85. Wooden sidewalks line **Allen Street★★**. Horse-drawn stagecoaches offer tours, shops sell Western 🚌 **souvenirs**. Saloons like the Crystal Palace are open for business. Gunslingers, gamblers and dance-hall hostesses wander the town of 1,570 citizens.

🚌 **Gunfights** are reenacted daily at the original **O.K. Corral** *(Allen St. between 3rd and 4th Sts.; 520-457-3456; www.ok-corral. com).* Other sights to see are the 1881 **Bird Cage Theatre** *(6th and Allen Sts.; 520-457-3421);* the **Rose Tree Inn** *(4th and Toughnut Sts.; 520-457-3326);* and **Tombstone Courthouse State Historic Park★** *(219 E. Toughnut St.; 520-457-3311; www.azparks.gov/Parks/TOCO).*

BISBEE★★

US-80 and Rte. 92, 96mi southeast of Tucson. 520-432-5421. www.bisbeearizona.com.

This historic **mining town**, its buildings clinging precariously to the sides of Tombstone Canyon, became the largest settlement between St. Louis and San Francisco after ore was discovered in 1877. The Copper Queen Mine closed in 1975—after $2 billion in copper, gold, lead, silver and zinc had been taken.

Today a significant number of Bisbee's 5,600 residents operate galleries, shops and coffeehouses within the late 19C and early 20C buildings of Italianate Victorian architecture.

The **Bisbee Mining and Historical Museum** *(5 Copper Queen Plaza; 520-432-7071; www.bisbeemuseum. org)* once served as the mining company's office.

The **Copper Queen Hotel** *(11 Howell Ave.; 520-432-2216; www.copperqueen.com)* has been the town's informal focal point since 1902.

Queen Mine Tours★★ *(US-80 to Historic Old Bisbee Exit; 520-432-2071; www.queenminetour.com)* are guided by retired miners. A 13mi bus tour visits the **Lavender Pit**, a massive open-pit mine.

DOUGLAS

US-80 and US-191, 119mi southeast of Tucson. 520-417-7344. www.douglasaz.org.

This old ranching and copper-smelting town of 18,000 inhabitants, borders Agua Prieta, Mexico, and boasts 335 buildings on the National Historic Register. The 1907 **Gadsden Hotel** *(1046 G Ave.; 520-364-4481; www. hotelgadsden.com)* shows off its neo-Renaissance lobby with a marble staircase and a 42ft **stained-glass mural**. Although historians doubt that the event ever occurred, locals still express unwavering belief in the legend that Mexican revolutionary **Pancho Villa** once rode his horse

up the lobby staircase. The **Grand Theatre**, at 1139 G Avenue, opened in 1919. Ginger Rogers, Anna Pavlova, and John Philip Sousa are but three of the stars who have graced the stage over the years. Though the theater has since fallen on hard times, civic leaders began an ambitious effort in the 1980s to save it, and the Grand is now in Phase III of a four-phase restoration plan.

The **Slaughter Ranch** *(6153 Geronimo Trail; 520-558-2474; www.slaughterranch.com; open Wed–Sun 10am–3pm; closed Jan 1 and Dec 25; $8)*, 16mi southeast, is a National Historic Landmark that recalls turn-of-the-20C **cattle ranching**. Of interest on the 300-acre site are an adobe ranch house, ice house, wash house, granary and commissary.

BENSON

I-10 Exits 302-306, 45mi east of Tucson. 520-586-4293. www.bensonvisitorcenter.com.

Founded in 1880 on the Southern Pacific railroad line, Benson grew as a copper-smelting center.

The **Benson Railroad Historic District** *(E. 3rd St.)* preserves late 19C buildings. Today Amtrak's Sunset Limited makes a stop in town *(4th St. and Patagonia)* en route from Los Angeles. Kartchner Caverns State Park *(opposite)* lies just 12mi southwest of town via Route 90; visitors to the cave frequently overnight in Benson, which has several area B&Bs, guest ranches, motels and RV parks. Stop in for breakfast at the **Horseshoe Cafe and Bakery** *(154 E. 4th St.; 520-586-2872)*, in business since 1936.

WILLCOX

I-10 Exit 340, 83mi east of Tucson.

Originally known as Maley's Camp, Willcox was founded in1880. With a population of 3,700, Willcox is best known as the one-time home of singing cowboy and film star Rex Allen. The **Rex Allen "Arizona Cowboy" Museum and Willcox Cowboy Hall of Fame** *(150 N. Railroad Ave.; 520-384-4583; www. rexallenmuseum.org)* celebrates Allen's career, and honors local

ranchers who have carried on Arizona's cowboy tradition. The event **Wings Over Willcox** *(third weekend in January)* spotlights the **sandhill cranes** that winter at Willcox Playa, a dry lake and adjacent marshland south and east of town. **Apple Annie's Orchard** *(2081 W Hardy Rd, 520-384-2084, www.appleannies.com),* a farm where visitors pick or purchase apples, peaches and other produce, is a popular destination in autumn harvest season.

EXCURSIONS

▷ *From Tucson*

Titan Missile Museum★

I-19 Exit 69, 25mi south of Tucson. 520-625-7736. www.titanmissile museum.org. (See Pima Museum, TUCSON for description).

Tumacácori National Historical Park★

I-19 Exit 29, 50mi south of Tucson. 520-398-2341. www.nps.gov/ tuma. Open year-round daily 9am–5pm $3.

The ever-ambitious Father Eusebio Francisco Kino founded a mission at Tumacácori in January 1691. It is the oldest of the Spanish missions established in present-day Arizona. In 1800 Franciscan clerics embarked on an ambitious construction program, hoping to build a church that would rival the widely celebrated "white dove of the desert," Mission San Xavier del Bac *(see TUCSON chapter).* Construction continued through

the early 1800s, and the ruins of this impressive structure are the centerpiece of the historical park at Tumacácori today.
In addition to the ruins and the peaceful grounds that surround them, a **museum** and visitor center focus on the significance of Father Kino and the Spanish missions in historical context.

▷ *From Benson*

Kartchner Caverns State Park★★

Rte. 90, 12mi southwest of Benson. 520-586-4100. azstateparks.com/ parks/kaca. Open year-round daily for two guided tours (1hr30min and 1hr45min; each $22.95); reservations strongly recommended (520-586-2283). $6/ vehicle, $3 individual (on foot or bicycle); entrance fee is waived for visitors reserving tours in advance. Closed Dec 25.

This huge "wet" limestone cave in the Whetstone Mountains

was discovered in 1974, but kept secret until 1988. Unveiled to the public in late 1999, the stunning cave, home to 2,000 bats, actively drips **stalactites** and grows **stalagmites**.

Visitors enter via the **Discovery Center**, which features exhibits and videos on cave geology; natural history and spelunking. Two separate **tours** are available; one includes one of the largest known (21ft-by .25in) "soda straws," and a 58ft column called Kubla Khan. The entire cave may rival New Mexico's Carlsbad Caverns in size.

Amerind Foundation Museum★

1mi east of I-10 Exit 318, Dragoon, 16mi east of Benson. 520-586-3666. www.amerind.org. Open year-round Tue–Sun 10am–4pm. $8.

A nonprofit archaeology institute, Amerind is devoted to studying native cultures from Alaska to Patagonia. Exhibits include beadwork, costumes, pottery, basketry, ritual masks, weapons, children's toys and clothing, and cover everything from Cree snowshoe-making tools to the finest 19C Navajo weavings. Designed by H.M. Starkweather and completed over 28 years (1931-59), the Spanish Colonial Revival buildings blend dramatically with the boulders of Texas Canyon.

◗ *From Willcox*

Chiricahua National Monument★★

Rte. 186, 37mi southeast of Willcox. 520-824-3560. www.nps.gov/chir. Open year-round daily. Visitor center open daily 8am–4pm; closed Thanksgiving Day and Dec 25. $5 (16 years old and older).

Chiricahua Apaches called this preserve the "Land of the Standing-up Rocks," a name that aptly describes the fantastic wilderness of sculptured columns, spires, grottoes and balanced rocks. The region became a national monument in 1924 after promotion by the Swedish-immigrant owners of the **Faraway Guest Ranch** ("so god-awful far away from everything"), now a historic property that is open to

Chiricahua National Monument

🐦 Birding in Southeast Arizona

With more than 500 species of birds living in or passing through the state during their seasonal migrations, Arizona is one of the top bird-watching destinations in the US. Southeast Arizona is particularly popular with birders because extremes in elevation create **multiple biosystems** where unusually diverse populations of birds thrive. South of Benson, the San Pedro River runs north and south through the **San Pedro Riparian National Conservation Area**. Nestled in the San Pedro valley, this habitat is home to some 100 resident species and 250 species of migrant and wintering birds, including Great Blue Herons, red-tailed hawks, great horned owls and purple martins. South of Sierra Vista in the Huachuca Mountains, the **Ramsey Canyon Preserve** is renowned primarily for 15 species of hummingbirds that can be observed there. Some 170 species frequent the preserve, such as hermit thrushes, sulphur-bellied flycatchers and yellow-eyed juncos. In the Sulphur Springs Valley, south of Willcox, marshes and dry lake beds attract sandhill cranes, as well as other migrating birds. Some 17mi east of Douglas, the **San Bernardino National Wildlife Refuge** is home to about 270 species of birds, including ringneck ducks, yellow warblers, blue grosbeaks, and peregrine falcons. For other birding sites, a calendar of events and other information, contact the **Southeastern Arizona Birding Observatory** *(520-432-1388, www.sabo.org)*.

the public for guided tours. From the entrance station, **Bonita Canyon Drive★★** rises 8mi, past a small visitor center, to spectacular **Massai Point** at 6,870ft high in the Chiricahua Range. More than 20mi of **hiking trails** extend to such unusual rock formations as Duck on a Rock and Totem Pole. Believed to have been formed 27 million years ago in the wake of a nearby volcanic eruption, the Chiricahuas harbor numerous rare birds.

🐦 Fort Bowie National Historic Site

Rte 186, 20mi southeast of Willcox. 520-847-2500. www.nps.gov/fobo. Open year-round daily. Visitor center open daily 8am–4:30pm; closed Thanksgiving Day and Dec 25.

Although the US took possession of Southern Arizona with the completion, in 1855, of the Gadsden Purchase (1853), the Chiricahua Apaches resisted American efforts to settle the territory until Geronimo finally surrendered to US forces in 1886. For 20 years, Fort Bowie—an isolated outpost in the Chiricahua Mountains—served as a base of operations for US Army forces. Today, the ruins of Fort Bowie bear silent witness to the fierce and bloody struggle for control of Southern Arizona. A 3mi round-trip hike leads visitors to the **ruins** of the fort and a **visitor center**, passing the remains of a station that served as a stop for the Butterfield Stage Coach, the Fort Bowie cemetery and an Apache wikiup along the way. The site is also an ideal destination for hikers and bird-watchers.

RESTAURANTS

Given the huge travel industry and the need for dining service to customers year-round, restaurants in Arizona, both independent and resort-based, are much in demand. Where there's constant demand, competition widens. To increase their clientele, the state's gourmet chefs have been perfecting Southwest and global cuisines over the past decades, and a growing number of restaurants now focus on ingredients from sustainable farms like chiles, goat cheese, mesquite beans, home-grown tomatoes and locally raised pork. Travelers wishing to experience the Heart of the Southwest in every possible aspect should make an effort to dine on authentic local foods as much as possible, and yes, that means cactus too.

Prices and Amenities

The restaurants listed below were selected for their ambience, locationand/or value for money. Rates indicate the average cost of an appetizer, an entrée and a dessert for one person (not including tax, gratuity or beverages). Most restaurants are open daily (except where noted) and accept major credit cards. Call for information regarding reservations, dress code and opening hours.

Luxury	**$$$$**	>$75
Expensive	**$$$**	$50 to $75
Moderate	**$$**	$25 to $50
Inexpensive	**$**	<$25

Cuisine

For many people, Arizona food brings to mind Sonoran burritos and tacos. But now, chefs are returning to the state's true roots, celebrating indigenous desert bounty originally cherished by Native Americans, plus plenty of locally sourced ingredients. Nopales (cactus pads) give an earthy texture to contemporary menus, chile peppers in a rainbow of colors add sizzle, and Papago tepary beans can be soothing when dotted with goat cheese from Fossil Creek (in the tiny town of Strawberry) or from Black Mesa (in Snowflake). Other dishes commonly found in the state are blue-corn pancakes, red tomato tortillas, and green tomatillos pounded into molcajete salsa. Piñon nuts come crusted on roast chipotle chicken, pomegranate seeds are sprinkled in salads, and masa is handcrafted from heritage stone-ground corn and made into succulent tamales. As for drinks, a real Arizona margarita is made with agave from the southern desert, Willcox apples make a sweet-tart cider, and vineyards both north and south produce excellent Arizona wines.

Reservations

Arizona's high season runs from October through April, and reservations are highly recommended for most restaurants at dinner. For headliner destinations such as Elements, Vincent on Camelback, Kai and Binkley's, it helps to call several days in advance. A few enormously popular eateries don't take reservations, so prepare for a wait (it's worth it!) at spots like Café Elote, The Farm Kitchen, and Los Dos Molinos.

MUST EAT

FLAGSTAFF AREA

Expensive

Cottage Place

$$$ **Contemporary**

126 W. Cottage Ave., Flagstaff. 928-774-8431. www.cottageplace.com. Dinner only. Closed Mon–Tue.

This 1909 bungalow qualifies as "a find," tucked away on the edge of the Southside neighborhood. For nearly two decades, chef-owner Frank Branham has brought a touch of Europe to Northern Arizona by featuring escargots, boeuf Bourguignonne, and elaborate tableside presentations of Chateaubriand or rack of lamb for two. Old brick walls, crisp linen tablecloths, and elegantly styled plates dressed in edible flowers and "hand-painted" sauces add to the thrill of discovery.

 Criollo Latin Kitchen

$$$ **Latin American**

16 N. San Francisco St., Flagstaff. 928-774-0541. www.criolllolatin kitchen.com.

Always abuzz with conversation, this intimate eatery in Flagstaff's compact downtown ensconces diners in a sleek setting of brick walls and colorful wall paintings; all its pine is locally harvested ponderosa. Drawing numerous ingredients from Arizona farms, entrées reflect a meld of Spanish-Latin flavors. Try the salmon tostada with goat cheese and black-bean spread, the signature paella with saffron-infused Calasparra rice, or the catfish tacos with jalapeno glaze.

A sister restaurant, **Brix**, is located just north of downtown at 413 N. San Francisco Street.

Heartline Cafe

$$$ **New American**

1610 W. US-89A, Sedona. 928-282-0785. www.heartlinecafe.com.

People travel from all over to visit this beloved eatery. The owners started with a stylish stucco building and added live music at night. Specials are barbecue or tapas fiestas, but the eclectic breakfast, lunch and dinner menu ranges from lemon crème stuffed French baguette toast to local pecan-crusted trout, tea smoked chicken dumplings, and grilled filet mignon smothered in *queso de cabra* and mole sauce.

René at Tlaquepaque

$$$ **Contemporary**

In Tlaquepaque Village, 336 Rte. 179, Sedona. 928-282-9225. www.rene-sedona.com.

This stylish restaurant opened in 1977, and instantly became a landmark for its baked French onion soup and signature rack of lamb, carved tableside amid rich fabrics, chocolate woods and white tablecloths. René remains a top choice for celebrating special occasions with specialties like Dover sole *à la meunière* and truffle-porcini ravioli in sherry cream sauce.

Criollo Latin Kitchen

©Gwen Cannon/Michelin

RESTAURANTS

Moderate

Bin 239
$$ **Italian, American**
239 N. Marina St., Prescott.
928-445-3855. www.bin239.com.
Closed Sun–Mon.
Bin's interior glows with the
warmth of a wood-burning brick
oven, from which issue pizzas
topped with creative combinations
like pulled pork-jalapeno. Entrées
include New York steaks. Munchies
mean stacked caprese and a good
but messy Reuben panini. The wine
menu offers global labels from
America, Europe, and unexpected
locales like Milagro, New Mexico.

☙ Café Elote
$$ **Mexican**
In Kings Ransom Inn, 771 Rte. 179,
Sedona. 928-203-0105. www.
elotecafe.com. Dinner only.
Closed Sun–Mon.
Chef Jeff Smedstad works with
quality ingredients that base
his authentic regional Mexican
specialties. Order the chile relleno
of fire-roasted Poblano stuffed
with gooey cheese and crunchy
vegetable-nut picadillo, topped
with corn crema and local Arizona
goat cheese. The living room cum
coffee shop-style space isn't fancy,
but in season, it's a battle to get in,
given the no-reservations policy.

El Gato Azul
$$ **Mexican**
316 W. Goodwin St., Prescott.
928-445-1070. www.elgatoazul
prescott.com.
It's a bright yellow and blue
stucco shrine to red and green
chiles, used generously in eclectic
global specialties like green chile
mac 'n' cheese or shrimp-chorizo

creole stew. Sample tapas at the
industrial-mod bar or outside in
the pleasant back patio.

Inexpensive

Cruiser's Cafe 66
$ **American**
233 W. Rte. 66, Williams. 928-635-
2445. www.cruisers66.com.
This 1950s-60s-style tourist haunt,
set up in a former gas station, is
decorated with Route 66 road
signs and neon light sculptures.
Outside seating is ideal for people-
watching. Beer is tasty microbrew
from the owners, Peasleys' Grand
Canyon Brewing Company. Diner
grub of messy burgers, chicken
fried steak and greasy-great cheese
fries is the way to go.

Cruiser's Cafe 66

©Gwen Cannon/Michelin

Macy's European Coffeehouse
$ **American, Mexican**
14 S. Beaver St., Flagstaff. 928-774-
2243. www.macyscoffee.net.
Macy's European Coffeehouse,
Bakery & Vegetarian Restaurant
began 30 years ago when Tim
Macy brought fair-trade coffee,
comfort food, vegan fare, and
communal ambience to this
downtown storefront. The bakery
beckons customers with French
éclairs. A breakfast must is Belgian
waffles, a tofu-walnut-cranberry

MUST EAT

salad at lunch, and a vegetarian mushroom-Swiss burger for dinner.

PHOENIX AREA

Luxury

Binkley's

$$$$ **Contemporary**
6920 E. Cave Creek Rd., Cave Creek. 480-437-1072. www. binkleysrestaurant.com. Dinner only. Closed Sun–Mon.
Chef Kevin Binkley has surprises in *amuse bouches* like tiny savory doughnuts with thyme, parmesan and bacon butter, served through the meal. Pristine ingredients and tweezer-perfect preparations create dishes like skate dressed in pickled scallion, Blue Lake beans, quince, baby carrots and key-lime spaetzle. Reservations are a must for the 50-seat, Southwestern-style dining room.

Cartwright's

$$$$ **Southwest**
6710 E. Cave Creek Rd., Cave Creek. 480-488-8031. www.cartwrightssonoran ranchhouse.com. Dinner only.
Owner Eric Flatt incorporates the desert's bounty in complex dishes celebrating hand-harvested prickly pear, jojoba seeds, mesquite beans and saguaro fruit. Native American staples like beef-elk-buffalo end up in meatloaf sharing the menu with mesquite-wood grilled salmon atop sweet potato-tortilla hash, wood-grilled chayote squash and avocado salsa with crispy yucca root. Dressing up is advised for this luxury-ranch dining experience.

Christopher's

$$$$ **Contemporary**
2502 E. Camelback Rd., Phoenix. 602-522-2344. christophersaz.com.
Whether it's fennel lobster in smoked crème fraiche, or a fork-and-knife cheeseburger, Chef Christopher Gross flaunts his superb French skills within a sleek dining space that induces high-style ambience. **Crush Lounge**, also offers delicacies from pied de cochon with sweetbreads to wood oven duck confit and fig pizza.

Kai

$$$$ **Southwest**
In Sheraton Wild Horse Pass Resort, 5594 Wild Horse Pass Blvd., Chandler. 602-385-5726. www. wildhorsepassresort.com. Dinner only. Closed Sun–Mon. Dress code.
Produce from Indian farms, local cactus and mesquite beans star in Kai's world-class dishes. Try the salad of sous-vide roots, asparagus and mushrooms with heirloom tomatoes, Cabrales cheese marbles, micro snips, candied local pecans and young beets. Plan to dress up for meals served by staff who orchestrate their movements like ballet. Tasting menu signatures include grilled tenderloin of tribal buffalo with cholla buds in saguaro blossom syrup.

Michael Dominick's Steakhouse

$$$$ **Steakhouse**
15169 N. Scottsdale Rd., Scottsdale. 480-272-7271. www.dominickssteakhouse.com.
The rooftop dining room, set around a reflection pool, is capped with a retractable roof. It's all about indulgence at this multi-million dollar shrine to prime beef, where

the meat is cut in-house and dry aged, then broiled at 1,600 degrees under a swath of butter. The seafood is well worth reeling in too; the Maine lobster arrives stuffed with Maryland crab.

Sassi
$$$$ Italian
10455 E. Pinnacle Peak Pkwy., Scottsdale. 480-502-9095. www.sassi.biz. Dinner only. Closed Mon.
Constructed in stone on 6 acres of Sonoran desert, this 250-seat restaurant cost $10 million to build. Inside and out, it evokes a Southern Italian setting, complete with a courtyard fountain. The menu from Christopher Nicosia is grand with *pappardelle verde* of handmade spinach pasta tossed with spicy pork ragu, herbed ricotta and pecorino, or roasted branzino served tail-on and blackened.

Vincent on Camelback
$$$$ French-Southwest
3930 E. Camelback Rd., Phoenix. 602-224-0225. www.vincentsoncamelback.com. Dinner only. Closed Sun.
For some 25 years, Chef Vincent Guerithault has been setting new standards for French cuisine, celebrating the classics (savory rosemary roasted rack of lamb nearly melts in the mouth with a hint of spicy pepper jelly), while introducing innovative Arizona-style twists (such as duck confit presented as a tamale studded with Anaheim chile and raisins). White tablecloths enhance the French-château setting. The cozy patios and peek-a-boo kitchen add to the relaxed vibe.

Expensive

Elements Restaurant
$$$ Asian Fusion
In Sanctuary Camelback Mountain, 5700 E. McDonald Dr., Paradise Valley. 480-607-2300. www. elementsrestaurant.com.
Chef Beau MacMillan and views from the floor-to-ceiling windows of this mountainside dining room compete. Ultimately the cuisine shines so bright that diners' focus on the plate. Fusion feats include Maine lobster *udon carbonara* with pancetta, oyster mushrooms, Thai basil and tomato jam.

La Hacienda
$$$ Mexican
In the Fairmont Scottsdale, 7575 E. Princess Dr., Scottsdale. 480-585-4848. www.fairmont.com/ scottsdale. Dinner only.
Even the most basic *queso fundido* tastes special in this Spanish mansion of soaring wood-beamed ceilings, beehive fireplaces and candelabras. Chef Richard Sandoval grew up in Mexico City and uses the real ingredients like Oaxaca, Chihuahua and Gouda cheeses and *chile morita* salsa for the cheese dip. Seared scallop and crispy pork belly are delicious partners on the plate, moistened in blood-orange glaze with pumpkin puree and orange tomatillo demi.

Litchfield's
$$$ American
In Wigwam Resort, 300 E. Wigwam Blvd., Litchfield Park. 623-935-3811. www.wigwamarizona.com. Dinner only.
The charm starts with the setting, anchored by an open kitchen, leather furniture and rustic wood,

MUST EAT

plus a coveted landscaped patio. It continues with farm-fresh cuisine, honoring local purveyors and its own on-site organic garden. Small plates brim with good things like Italian sausage-white bean-mustard green soup, but entrées deserve contemplation too, for updated cowboy statements such as a hearty wood-fired pork chop paired with Hayden Mills polenta fries, house pickles and tobacco onions in white cheddar emulsion and rice wine molasses.

Noca
$$$ Italian
3118 E. Camelback Rd., Phoenix. 602-956-6622. restaurantnoca.com. Closed Mon in summer.
Owner Elliott Wexler is obsessive about ingredients, sourcing lobster from French Laundry supplier Ingrid Bengis, and tuna from Tokyo's famed Tsukiji Fish Market. Yet forget pretension, since alongside exquisite, handcrafted orecchiette beef short rib ragu you'll find mouthwatering fried chicken. There's also a family friendly Sunday Supper with mac 'n' cheese and cookies 'n' milk.

Prado
$$$ Mediterranean
In Montelucia Resort & Spa, 4949 E. Lincoln Dr., Scottsdale. 480-627-3004. www.montelucia.com.
A meal of tapas like antipasti showcasing house-cured salumi and local honeycomb, or a full dinner of wood-roasted chicken and Brussels sprouts glazed in pecan butter? It's best to order both, and pair them with cocktails like a Brazilian blackberry Caipirinha—a blend of Sagatiba rum, blackberry puree, lime and

soda. The Moorish-style interior shows off opulent tilework and carved wood; the pleasant patio is framed by flowers and views of Camelback Mountain.

Old Town Tortilla Factory
$$$ Southwest
6910 E. Main St., Scottsdale. 480-945-4567. www.oldtown tortillafactory.com. Dinner only.
This longstanding cantina is popular for its secluded fountain patio as well as its margaritas and tequilas. Fresh tortillas, made daily in two dozen flavors, undergird a creative gourmet menu of updated dishes like chips 'n' dip of roasted corn, peppers, onions, tomatoes, avocado and cilantro lime in fresh blue crab and creamy garlic. Beneath cathedral ceilings, servers present upscale dishes like pork chops with an Ancho-raspberry sauce and wild-mushroom tacos.

Wright's at the Biltmore
$$$ Contemporary
In Arizona Biltmore, 2400 E. Missouri Ave., Phoenix. 602-955-6600. www.arizonabiltmore.com. Dinner and Sunday brunch only.
The Frank Lloyd Wright-inspired architecture creates an elegant environment for sophisticated dining. Spartan and crisp, the furnishings—blonde wood tables coupled with wood and leather chairs—evoke Wright's interiors. Dishes can be customized for small or large portions, and wine pairings are offered with each, like beef Wellington with Sonoma Merlot, or salmon rillettes sprinkled in sea-salt capers, egg, crème fraiche, chive and caviar with sparkling wine, as examples.

Moderate

Barrio Queen

$$ **Mexican/Latin American**

*7114 E. Stetson Dr., Scottsdale. 480
-656-4197. www.barrioqueen.com.*
An actual barrio queen runs this
colorful shrine adorned in Day
of the Dead decor. Chef-owner
Silvana Salcido Esparza grew up
baking *pan de Manteca* for her
family's business. Yet her layering
of flavors is almost European,
spiked with uncommon accents
like piñon cream slathered on
savory roast chicken. Elaborate
recipes include Oaxacan/
Chihuahuan filet mignon with
Serrano ham, menonita cheese,
sautéed huitlacoche and fried egg
in a port-Serrano reduction.

Beckett's Table

$$ **American**

*3717 E. Indian School Rd., Phoenix.
602-954-1700. www.beckettstable.
com. Dinner only. Closed Mon.*
Home cooking was never quite
so refined until chef-owner Justin
Beckett trotted out his salute
to Americana with chicken 'n'
dumplings with parsnips and
butternut in herbed saffron cream.
The setting is industrial gastropub,
while the food is pure happiness
in the belly, including Schreiner's
sausage dunked in creamy grits,
bacon cheddar biscuits glazed in
candied jalapeño orange butter,
and melt-in-the-mouth short ribs
over mashed potatoes.

Le Chalet

$$ **French**

*5626 W. Bell Rd., Glendale.
602-337-8760. lechalet-llc.com.*
The star here is the tartines,
snackable beauties of open-
face sandwiches topped in
savories such as grilled chicken
breast, grilled onions, Swiss and
mozzarella, or a delightful layering
of crispy bacon, onion, raclette
cheese, mozzarella and béchamel.
Crepes are another specialty,
prepared tableside, on tables
made from wine barrels.

Citizen Public House

$$ **Contemporary**

*7111 E. 5th Ave., Scottsdale.
480-398-4208. www.citizen
publichouse.com. Dinner only.*
Bernie Kantak first wowed Valley
diners as chef at Cowboy Ciao, and
now he's got his own show in this
eclectic-styled pub. The homey-chic
dark wood setting is welcoming,
featuring the chef's family photos.
The bar scene rocks, as any good
pub should. Playful dishes like
chicken 'n' waffles drizzled in blue
clover honey, and meatloaf infused
with Montenegro Amaro Italian
liqueur are among his fanciful
choices. Desserts come from local
pastry magician Tracy Dempsey -
the bag o' bacon brittle is addictive.

El Encanto

$$ **Mexican**

*6248 E. Cave Creek Rd.,
Cave Creek. 480-488-1752.
www.elencantorestaurants.com.*
Bill Nelson opened this Mission
church-style cantina in 1989,
building warrens of colorfully
decorated rooms around a
courtyard set with a large pond
occupied by resident ducks. It's still
operated by the family today, with
the same, soul-satisfying Sonoran
staples of spicy chile verde
scooped up with hot tortillas,
handmade tamales, and signature
pollo fundido of a big, juicy

chicken breast rolled in a flour tortilla, fried crispy and smothered in tongue tingling jalapeno cream cheese sauce and cheddar.

Local Bistro
$$ **Italian**
20581 N. Hayden Rd.,
Scottsdale. 480-302-6050.
www.localbistroaz.com.
Chef-owner Andrea Volpi has been a Valley legend since he opened his first restaurant in1994. He's known for handcrafted pastas, cheeses, and authentic specialties like "drunken" bread of crusty loaf splashed with white wine, layered with gruyere and prosciutto, then broiled. His latest spot is a family-friendly trattoria, yet it's still Slow Food worthy, given wood-fired Neapolitan-style pizzas topped in fontina, wild mushrooms, arugula and truffle oil, or primavera risotto with the seasons best vegetables.

The Mission
$$ **Latin American**
3815 N. Brown Ave., Scottsdale.
480-636-5005. www.themission
az.com. Dinner only.
Leave it to innovative chef Matt Carter to put a new twist on traditional South of the Border delights like crispy pork, crafted of pork belly marinated in cola, lime, chiltepin pepper and peanut. Pink Himalayan salt blocks form the bar's wall, sparkling chandeliers brighten the antique furniture, and mouthwatering signatures such as green chile duck confit atop cheesy fried hominy and smoked mushrooms in Sultana grape-Serrano-peanut mole light up the menu.

Los Dos Molinos
$ **Mexican**
8646 S. Central Ave., Phoenix.
602-243-9113. www.losdosmolinos
phoenix.com. Closed Sun–Mon.
Diners in search of taste bud thrills flock to this colorful eatery that looks like a Mission church outside and raises an altar to fiery Hatch chiles within. The Chavez family has been cooking their wickedly spicy New Mexican chile-pumped *carne adovada* for more than two decades. Regulars throng the place for its blue corn tamales, red-chile burros (think burritos), and gutsy garlic shrimp, while dousing the heat with potent margaritas.

 The Farm Kitchen at South Mountain
$ **American**
6106 S. 32nd St., Phoenix.
602-276-6545. www.thefarm
atsouthmountain.com. Lunch
only. Closed Mon.
Here, it's old-time agricultural Arizona, sitting on the brick patio in the shade of pecan trees, and eating artisan sandwiches, soups and salads based on ingredients grown in the organic fields mere steps away. The BBQ sandwich features local pork from The Meat Shop nearby, while the Cobb salad is a salute to Arizona purveyors, showcasing slow-roasted turkey, Meat Shop bacon, Hickman's Family Farms hard boiled egg, McClendon's Select Farm Campari tomatoes, local pecans and crumbled bleu cheese.

RESTAURANTS

Uncle Sam's

$ American

18913 N. 83rd Ave., Peoria. 623-362-3900. www.unclesamsaz.com. Other locations in Phoenix and Scottsdale.

Anyone who doesn't think sub sandwiches are exciting has never been to this friendly joint owned by the Frimmel family. Since 1980, nearly 2,000 customers a day flock to the eatery for mile-high sandwiches, crisp-crusted pizzas, stromboli, calzones, wings, salads, hoagies and grinders stuffed with premium deli meats and cheeses. Cheesesteaks are dangerously delicious, too, overstuffed with combos of steak or chicken, cheese, pizza sauce, green peppers, mushrooms, onions and hot or sweet peppers.

TUCSON AREA

Expensive

🍴 Cafe Roka

$$$ American Fusion

35 Main St., Bisbee. 520-432-5153. www.caferoka.com. Dinner only. Reservations recommended.

Owner-chef Rod Kass took a notorious dive in Bisbee and transformed it into a bistro that is elegant and comfortable. Meals combine elements of Italian, Mediterranean and Californian cuisines: four-course dinners include soup, salad, sorbet and entrée. Although the menu changes seasonally, the roasted half duck has been a mainstay from the start, as have been pasta and vegetarian dishes, including the ever-popular vegetarian lasagna. The balcony tables are especially pleasant.

Downtown Kitchen + Cocktails

$$$ International

135 S. 6th Ave., Tucson. 520-623-7700. www.downtownkitchen.com. No lunch Sat–Sun.

Janos Wilder is arguably the most prominent, and perhaps best-loved, chef in Southern Arizona. Having closed his signature restaurant at La Paloma Resort, he has returned to his roots in Tucson. Located in a newly resurgent central business district, the airy dining room is lined with exposed brick walls; sidewalk tables offer seating out front. Entrées include red-curry catfish, maple-brined pork loin or grilled eggplant with house-pulled mozzarella.

Moderate

Blue Willow

$$ New American

2616 N. Campbell Ave., Tucson. 520-327-7757. wwwbluewillowtucson.com

Though it started as a bakery and breakfast cafe, Blue Willow is now a full-fledged bistro offering breakfast, brunch, lunch and dinner. The eggs Benedict, huevos rancheros and chorizo scramble are breakfast favorites, and one dinner standout is savory meatloaf made with local, grass-fed beef. The 1940 adobe home that houses the restaurant is complete with covered patio, a popular spot.

🍴 Cafe Poca Cosa

$$ Mexican

110 E. Pennington St., Tucson. 520-622-6400. www.cafepocacosa tucson.com. Closed Sun and Mon.

Housed in a sleek setting with polished metal and pomegranate walls, Tucson's premier Mexican restaurant features imaginative food from all over Mexico, including 26 varieties of mole. Owner Suzana Davila hails from Guaymas, Sonora, and her mix of traditional and innovative recipes has captured national attention. Dining is like unwrapping a Christmas present, since the chalkboard menu changes twice daily. But look for favorites like *relleno carne y salsa blanca, lomo de puerco con chile ancho ciruela,* and *pastel de elote con crema de betabel.*

Inexpensive

Bisbee Breakfast Club
$ American, Mexican
75 Erie St., Bisbee. 520-432-5885.
www.bisbeebreakfastclub.com.
Breakfast and lunch only.
The old-time mining town purrs with nostalgia, and so does this retro, turquoise and tile landmark. The cooks sling delicious breakfast belly fillers, like the Wingdinger, bringing a skillet of hash browns loaded with melted Jack cheese eggs and spicy sausage gravy. Hearty lunches include the Huckburger smothered in shaved ham, Swiss, and homemade Jim Beam BBQ sauce.

El Guero Canelo
$ Mexican
5201 South 12th Ave., Tucson.
520-295-9005. elguerocanelo.com.
This south-side restaurant is widely credited as one of the originators of the "Sonoran hot dog," a Tucson fast-food specialty that wraps an oversize hot dog in a Mexican bun, with onions, bacon, hot sauce, tomatoes and beans ladled on top. The restaurant's tacos and burros (large, handheld burritos

in flour tortillas) are also favorites. El Guero has newer locations in the city's north and east sides, but aficionados prefer the original south side location.

El Minuto Cafe
$ Mexican
354 South Main Ave., Tucson.
www.elminutocafe.com.
Awash in local color, this restaurant sits at the edge of downtown's historic barrio. In business since 1939, the corner cafe draws in patrons, many of them regulars, for plates of traditional Sonoran mainstays like tacos, enchiladas and burros; but chimichangas, chiles rellenos and spicy Mexican soups are the specialties of the house. The outdoor patio, hung with festive lights, makes a pleasant spot for dinner. The cafe is an easy walk from the Tucson Convention Center.

WEST ARIZONA

Expensive

Shugrue's
$$$ American
1425 N. McCulloch Blvd., Lake Havasu City. 928-453-1400.
www.shugrues.com/lakehavasu.
Overlooking the London Bridge, Shugrue's specializes in seafood. It also knows steaks, and slathers them in classic sauces. Continental staples include chicken sautéed with shrimp, artichokes, mushrooms, tomatoes and white wine. The Shugrue family is an Arizona legend for their many restaurants; this one dates back 20 years, but still feels fresh, thanks to a sleek design and a busy bar.

HOTELS

Whether it's a quaint B&B in a tiny mountain town, or a big-city luxury resort boasting world class restaurants, a golf course and a spa, Arizona's accommodations are varied and impressive, appealing to travelers of all kinds. Put your feet up in a rustic log cabin next to a gurgling creek, or stretch out in an opulent Asian-chic retreat where a seasoned Iron Chef prepares gourmet meals. No matter where you overnight, the bonus in the Grand Canyon State is always the outdoors, offering breathtaking views, and activities from hiking and fishing to, well, just stargazing.

Prices and Amenities

The properties listed below were selected for their ambience, location and/or value for money. Price categories reflect the average cost for a standard double room for two people in winter's high season, not including taxes or surcharges. Travelers with the freedom (and gumption) to visit Arizona in the summer can benefit from hotel discounts of sometimes as much 50 percent, except in the northern areas of the state.

Luxury	$$$$$	> $350
Expensive	$$$$	$250-$350
Moderate	$$$	$175-$250
Inexpensive	$$	$100-$175
Budget	$	< $100

Reservations

Advance reservations are highly recommended for all Arizona's lodgings, be they resorts, hotels, bed-and-breakfast inns, hostels or campgrounds, especially in the state's winter season. Reservations for accommodations at very popular attractions like Grand Canyon National Park should be made as far in advance as possible (13 months ahead). Reservations can generally be made online on the individual property's website with a credit card.

FLAGSTAFF AREA

Expensive

🏨 L'Auberge de Sedona
$$$$ 87 rooms
301 L'Auberge Ln., Sedona.
928-282-1661 or 800-905-5745.
www.lauberge.com.
Following a $25 million renovation in 2011, this landmark property of 1984 is updated with 30 new luxury cottages and suites, a new saltwater pool, upgraded 5,000sq ft spa, and sleek new lobby. The cottages have a country-French feel; the new Vista Suites are Zen-like retreats with balconies, outdoor cedar showers and fireplaces. **L'Auberge Restaurant (\$\$\$\$)** serves Mediterranean flavors in three- or four-course tasting menus. The new Veranda lounge adds extra patio seating.

Enchantment Resort
$$$$ 218 rooms
525 Boynton Canyon Rd., Sedona.
928-282-2900 or 800-826-4180.
www.enchantmentresort.com.
Low-profile adobe-style casitas with beehive fireplaces and private balconies nestle against red rocks. A $25 million renovation in 2012 brings high-profile style to the legendary property, where

expansive suites, some with kitchenettes and private pools, are done in lavish style with Native American art. The spa's specialty is Native American earth-clay wraps. The new **Che-Ah-Chi Restaurant ($$$$)** impresses with contemporary American-Southwestern cuisine.

Moderate

Briar Patch Inn
$$$ 19 cabins
3190 N. State Rte. 89A, Sedona. 928-282-2342. www.briarpatch inn.com.
This charming retreat, built on 9 acres in the mid-1940s, hugs the banks of Oak Creek. Lodgepole Southwestern-style cottages come with full kitchens, and creekside hammocks hung beneath the shade of oaks and sycamores. Guests enjoy massage and yoga, the inn's private swimming holes and a hearty buffet breakfast that includes a daily quiche.

El Portal
$$$ 12 suites
97 Portal Ln., Sedona, 800-313-0017. www.elportalsedona.com.
Each of the dozen luxury suites is appointed with authentic 1900-1930s Southwestern furniture placed within whitewashed adobe walls and on Saltillo floors. A personal concierge plans custom hiking and jeep tours, or books guests' spa privileges at **Los Abrigados Resort** next door. Fido-friendly rooms offer private stone courtyards. Breakfast is an additional charge, but can be enjoyed en-suite, featuring double cream French brie, bacon and raspberry chipotle omelets.

Garland's Lodge
$$$ 16 cabins
8067 N. State Rte. 89A, Oak Creek Canyon. 928-282-3343. www.garlandslodge.com. Closed mid-Nov–late Mar.
This historic property usually books a year in advance. Spread across 10 acres, it's an oasis of organic gardens, apple orchards, and cozy 1930s log cabins. Each comes with quilted beds, fireplaces, and creekside views. The Lodge restaurant sits in the original homestead (early 1900s), and now serves breakfast (think buttermilk pumpkin waffles) afternoon tea, and four-course dinners like roast chicken with wild mushrooms—all included in the rate.

The Inn at 410 B&B
$$$ 8 rooms
410 N. Leroux St., Flagstaff. 928-774-0088. www.inn410.com.
The 19C Craftsman-style home brims with nice cuddly things, like fireplaces, down blankets, feather pillows, rubber duckies for the spa tubs, and has a gay-friendly vibe. Each room sports its own theme; the Southwest suite has a kiva fireplace, and original brick walls dating to 1894. Breakfast means baked apple custard French toast, and lemon ricotta pancakes.

Inexpensive

Grand Canyon Railway Hotel
$$ 298 rooms
23 N. Grand Canyon Blvd., Williams. 928-635-4010. www.thetrain.com.
Built in the late 1990s, this motor-type hotel was designed to recall an old train-depot hotel opened by the Santa Fe Railroad as a Harvey

House. It's a convenient location for passengers taking the train to the canyon. The large, welcoming lobby has a massive stone fireplace and cushy seating. Standard rooms are spacious, and have full bathrooms with tub and shower.

Hotel Monte Vista
$$ 50 rooms
100 N. San Francisco St., Flagstaff. 928-779-6971 or 800-545-3068. www.hotelmontevista.com.
Built in 1926 to service the Santa Fe Railroad Depot, this four-story grand dame lured famous guests like Humphrey Bogart, Clark Gable and Zane Grey. Antiques fill nooks and crannies; the historic charm is palpable. Room have private bath, and are amply sized, with luxuries like Oriental rugs. The retro lounge offers billiards and live music.

🏛 La Posada
$$ 48 rooms
303 E. 2nd St., Winslow. 928-289-4366. www.laposada.org.
Located east of Flagstaff, La Posada was Fred Harvey's last achievement, opened in 1930 as a Spanish hacienda that became a favorite retreat for Hollywood stars.

Closed for 40 years, it reopened in 1997, with individually decorated rooms, an art-filled lobby, multi-level lounges, secret hallways and sculpture-filled gardens. Suites feature carved-wood furniture and four poster canopy beds as well as original mosaic-tile bathrooms. **The Turquoise Room ($$$)** serves up contemporary Southwestern dishes like spicy cassoulet stocked with local churro lamb, duck leg and elk sausage over Tohono O'odham tepary beans and chiles.

Surgeon's House B&B
$$ 4 apartments
101 Hill St., Jerome. 800-639-1452. www.surgeonshouse.com.
When the historic Spanish-style house was built in 1916, it was as the home of the chief surgeon of the small mining town. Now it's an eclectic hillside bed and breakfast inn, with soaring views of Verde Valley's wine country. Rooms are spacious and charming, and feature hardwood floors, private baths and balconies or patios. The breakfast buffet sets the appetite for a day of wine tasting, with elegant dishes like crab frittata and home-baked scones.

Grand Canyon Railway Hotel

©Grand Canyon Railway

Budget

Annabel Inn

$ **3 rooms**
611 N. Seventh St., Cottonwood.
928-649-3038. www.theannabe
linn.com.

A French-country cottage with
eco-friendly statements—in the
middle of a historic mining town?
True, since the area has developed
its Winery Trail, you'll toast this
gracious European-style B&B, just
southwest of Sedona, for its French
and Italian antique furnishings,
gourmet breakfasts that include
espresso from Italy, caviar and
chocolates, plus concierge service.

Molly Butler Lodge & Molly's Cabin Keepers

$ **50 cabins, 3 rooms**
109 Main St., Greer. 928-735-7617.
www.mollybutlerlodge.com.
Since 1910 the historic lodge has
welcomed visitors to its 8,500ft
hideaway in the White Mountains,
near New Mexico. The lodge is cozy
with wood paneling; the scattered
cabins range in style from cowboy
"condos" to million-dollar estates,
with amenities like 🛁 **hot tubs**, a
billiards room and home theaters.
The **Lodge Restaurant ($$)** serves
American classics such as slow-
roasted prime rib and apple pie.

NORTHEAST ARIZONA

Inexpensive

Holiday Inn Canyon de Chelly

$$ **108 rooms**
Indian Rte. 7, just east of Chinle.
928-674-5000 or 888-465-4329.
www.holidayinn.com.
In an area with extremely limited
lodging facilities, this inn just

outside the entrance to Canyon de
Chelly National Park is a pleasant
surprise. Its adobe design blends
in well with its surroundings in a
canyon-bottom cottonwood grove.
There's a pool, and the on-site
restaurant serves decent Navajo
dishes such as lamb stew. It's also
closest to the park, and well past
the highway sprawl of Chinle.

PHOENIX AREA

Luxury

Hyatt Regency Scottsdale Resort and Spa

$$$$$ **492 rooms**
7500 E. Doubletree Ranch Rd.,
Scottsdale. 480-444-1234 or
800-233-1234. www.scottsdale.
hyatt.com.

A "water playground" (with 10
pools, a 3-story waterslide and
sand beach) anchors this 27-acre
resort. Guests relax in certified
hypo-allergenic "respire" one-
bedrooms with balconies, or ultra-
luxury, lakeside casitas suites with
fireplaces and rooftop decks. They
also have access to three private
club golf courses. **Alto Ristorante
E Bar ($$$)** features Italian dinners
that include a Venetian gondola
ride on the lagoon. The Japanese
omakase-theme **Noh ($$$)** seats
just six people.

Royal Palms Resort and Spa

$$$$$ **119 rooms**
5200 E. Camelback Rd., Phoenix.
602-840-3610 or 800-672-6011.
www.royalpalmshotel.com.
This intimate, secluded resort at
the foot of Camelback Mountain,
was built in Spanish-Colonial style
in 1929. It appeals to couples with
custom perks like champagne

Casita, Hermosa Inn

balloon rides. The spa offers a body buff and facial using local fruit. The original mansion houses **T. Cook's ($$$$)**, serving Mediterranean cuisine from a wood-burning fireplace, and set in an Old-World salon rich with brick, tapestries and soft-lit chandeliers.

Expensive

The Boulders
$$$$ 223 rooms
34631 N. Tom Darlington Dr., Carefree. 480-488-9009 or 888-579-2631. www.theboulders.com.
Towering red boulders dotting this world-class resort north of Scottsdale are just part of the allure. Two 18-hole championship golf courses, the Golden Door spa and eight tennis courts complete the siren call. Gambel's quail strut the pathways, and a few owls nest outside the luxury Southwest-style casitas. Four swimming pools await guests' emergence.

Hermosa Inn
$$$$ 34 rooms
5532 N. Palo Cristi Rd., Paradise Valley. 602-955-8614 or 800-241-1210. www.hermosainn.com.

Cowboy artist Lon Megargee built this 1930s hacienda; today his portraits grace the restaurant. Casitas are spread over six acres of prickly pear and barrel cacti; an adobe spa casa sits in the back. Aged chaps hung on walls create a ranch atmosphere, while wine and charcuterie service on the private patios smacks of modern luxury. The original house is now **Lon's at the Hermosa ($$$$)**, presenting "Artful American" cuisine such as a savory Three Little Pigs plate of loin, braised cheek, crisp belly, asparagus, polenta and applesauce.

Moderate

CopperWynd Resort & Club
$$$ 40 rooms and villas
13225 N. Eagle Ridge Dr., Fountain Hills. 480-333-1900. www.copperwynd.com.
This boutique luxury inn tucked in the McDowell Mountains offers dramatic views, a full-service spa, 2 swimming pools, 9 tennis courts and a 5,000sq ft fitness center. Rooms are done in European decor. **Alchemy Restaurant and Wine Bar ($$$)** serves New

American cuisine with Arizona accents in plates like duck breast with butternut squash ravioli, string beans, sundried cranberries and candied pecans.

Ritz-Carlton, Phoenix

$$$ **281 rooms and suites**
2401 E. Camelback Rd., Phoenix. 602-468-0700. www.ritzcarlton.com.
Eleven floors tower over the heart of the Camelback Corridor, offering executive amenities and resort-style perks that include an outdoor, upper-deck swimming pool overlooking the city. The decor is antique European, and the service is white glove, including a club level for private concierge and culinary-cocktail services. Guests dine at breakfast, lunch and dinner in **Bistro 24 ($$)**, enjoying American regional cuisine with a French accent, in dishes like steel-cut oatmeal brûlée, a crab-cake sandwich, and steak au poivre.

Inexpensive

Hotel San Carlos

$$ **128 rooms**
202 N. Central Ave., Phoenix. 602-253-4121 or 866-253-4121. www.hotelsancarlos.com.
A downtown staple since 1928, this classic yellow-brick high rise is an anomaly in a land of sprawling spa resorts and cozy golf haciendas. Chandeliers and period wallpaper give an Old-World ambience to common spaces; black and white photographs and Western paintings grace the guest corridors. Five signature suites are named for Mae West, Marilyn Monroe and other stars. Off the lobby, the Ghost Lounge plays off its "haunted" legend. The surprise is a modern rooftop pool.

Sheraton Wild Horse Pass Resort & Spa

$$ **500 rooms**
5594 W. Wild Horse Pass Blvd., Chandler. 602-225-0100. www.wildhorsepassresort.com.
Designed in the style of the Gila River Indian Community's 372,000-acre reservation upon which it sits, and anchored by a mini "Colorado River," this resort is a salute to traditional Arizona. Yet the sprawling property is completely modern, including the 17,500sq ft **Aji Spa**, two 18-hole golf courses, 4 waterfall pools, and an equestrian center for rides in the wild-horse preserve. At the internationally acclaimed **Kai** restaurant **($$$$)**, French-trained staff present indigenous feasts like red deer venison in spiced sweet chile.

The Wigwam Resort

$$ **331 rooms and suites**
300 E. Wigwam Blvd., Litchfield Park. 623-935-3811 or 800-327-0396. www.wigwamresort.com.
Built in 1918 as a private retreat for Goodyear Tire executives, the posh property was turned into a resort in 1929. Casita-style guest rooms sit amid flower gardens and graceful palm trees. Highlights include 3 swimming pools with two 25-ft waterslides, 54 holes of championship golf, tennis courts, and an on-site Elizabeth Arden Red Door Spa. Flagship restaurant **Litchfield's ($$$)** serves farm-fresh cuisine in updated statements such as a wood-fired pork chop with Hayden Mills polenta fries.

HOTELS

TUCSON AREA

Luxury

Canyon Ranch

$$$$$ 110 rooms
8600 E. Rockcliff Rd., Tucson.
520-749-9000 or 800-742-9000.
www.canyonranch.com.
This high-profile, all-inclusive
luxury spa opened in 1979 to
help inaugurate the idea of long,
European-style restorative retreats.
Stucco casitas are scattered
amid 150 acres of desert in the
Santa Catalina foothills, lavishly
landscaped with flowers, cactus
gardens and fountains. At the
heart of the ranch is the 80,000sq
ft spa. Activities include 40 daily
fitness classes, a high-ropes course,
climbing wall and zipline. Three
healthy gourmet meals a day are
served in the Spanish Colonial-
style clubhouse.

Expensive

Arizona Inn

$$$$ 95 rooms
2200 E. Elm St., Tucson.
520-325-1541 or 800-933-1093.
www.arizonainn.com.
Little has changed since Franklin
Roosevelt came to "rough it" in the
1930s at this hacienda-style hotel.
Even the family ownership remains
the same. Velvet spans of grass
surround pink casitas with patios
on 14 acres of carefully tended
gardens shared with a pool, clay
tennis courts and croquet lawns.
The **Dining Room ($$$$)** features
creative American cuisine beneath
its cathedral ceiling, with dishes
like branzino pan-seared over
Forbidden rice and red Swiss chard
in lemon grass beurre blanc and

tomato chile jam. In winter,
afternoon tea is served in the
comfortable library.

Westward Look Wyndham Grand Resort and Spa

$$$$ 241 rooms
245 E. Ina Rd., Tucson.
520-297-1151 or 800-722-2500.
www.westwardlook.com.
An artful cross between a guest
ranch and a leisure resort,
Westward Look resides on a
ridge beneath the Santa Catalina
Mountains. Luxury casitas dot
the 80-acre grounds, offering
views from every room. Trails are
designed for hiking and riding.
The spa focuses on desert-theme
remedies like the Abyhanga
massage ritual. Flagship restaurant
Gold ($$$) incorporates fresh
produce from the chef's garden
in contemporary American dishes
like chorizo-stuffed pork chop in
pineapple-kumquat chutney.

Moderate

JW Marriott Starr Pass Resort & Spa

$$$ 575 rooms, 35 suites
3800 W. Starr Pass Blvd., Tucson.
520-792-3500. www.jwmarriott
starrpass.com.
The resort's scale is large, but laid
out so that each room includes a
private patio or balcony.
The main attractions are the water
features: a 177,000-gallon lazy
river with two islands, 22 misting
fountain jets, a water slide, and
four pools. Golf is another option,
and kids love the Blur Teen Lounge
with video games. For dinner
Primo ($$$$) sources its own
organic garden and Tohono O'dam
Nation ranches for indigenous

Westward Look Wyndham Grand Resort and Spa

specialties like pan-seared cobia in silky corn sauce.

Inexpensive

Desert Diamond Casino Hotel
$$ **151 rooms and suites**
7350 S. Nogales Hwy., Tucson. 520-294-7777. www.ddcaz.com.
The Tohono O'odham Nation hits the jackpot with this luxury 320,000sq ft, $90 million hotel and casino that boasts more than 170,000sq ft for slot machines, blackjack and poker tables. It's all about fun, from the multiple concert-caliber stages and swimming pools to dinner at **The Steak House ($$$)**, where the exhibition kitchen sends out elegant chophouse plates like Himalayan salt brick ahi or beef filet with lump crab.

Loews Ventana Canyon
$$ **398 rooms, 26 suites**
7000 N. Resort Dr., Tucson. 520-299-2020. www.loewshotels.com.
Private balconies for every room provide lovely views of the Santa Catalina Mountains, while two golf PGA courses and a hiking trail punctuated by an 80ft waterfall

place guests happily in the great outdoors. The 7,000sq ft Lakeside Spa is another hallmark, offering Arizona-themed treatments such as the Sedona Sacred Ritual of a cedar wood-citrus-desert salt full-body scrub, and a Sedona clay body mask with purifying white sage smoke, backdropped by ceremonial Native American music.

SOUTHEAST ARIZONA

Inexpensive

🐦 Casa de San Pedro B&B
$$ **10 rooms**
8933 S. Yell Ln., Hereford. 520-366-1300. www.bedandbirds.com.
Set on 10 acres next to the San Pedro River and Riparian National Conservation Area near Bisbee, this inn boasts some of the best bird-watching in Arizona. Picture an Old-World style setting reminiscent of Spain and Mexico, with hand-painted tile, against the backdrop of the Huachuca Mountain canyons. Cooking classes by professional guest chefs master dishes like chicken pâté and pineapple tarte tatin. The included breakfast features eggs Benedict

151

Presidential Suite Bedroom, Loews Ventana Canyon

©Loews Ventana Canyon

atop lavosh, for example. A slice of afternoon pie is complimentary.

🐾 Copper Queen Hotel
$$ **52 rooms**
11 Howell Ave., Bisbee. 520-432-2216. www.copperqueen.com.
Built in 1902 as the hub of a copper-mining metropolis, this landmark property still rivets visitors' attention with its eclectic Italian-Victorian style, cathedral ceilings and large antique safe behind the oak front desk. Completely renovated, all rooms have modern amenities, yet period furnishings maintain the turn-of-the-century charm. Celebrities such as Marlon Brando and Julia Roberts have enjoyed the hillside views from the pool.

Esplendor Resort
$$ **179 rooms, 13 suites**
1069 Camino Caralampi, Rio Rico. 520-281-1901. www.esplendor-resort.com.
Secluded south of Tucson near the Tubac art colony, this resort brims with elegant whimsy in unique suite decor showcasing cowboys, Indian teepees, a Victorian bordello, or standard Southwestern style rooms with private patios or balconies. The golf course meanders along cottonwood and mesquite tree-lined fairways.
San Cayetano Restaurant ($$$) features Primal Grill TV star chef Steven Raichlen in a continental menu including food items from the show.

Sonoita Inn
$$ **18 rooms**
3243 Hwy. 82 at 83, Sonoita. 520-455-5935. www.sonoitainn.com.
It's an odd place for a salute to Secretariat, complete with a reproduction of the famed racehorse's barn, but the inn's original owner, the Carmichael family, owned the Virginia farm where Secretariat was foaled. Now, Sonoita, 50mi southeast of Tucson, is a top wine-producing region, so the two have come together. The inn serves a horse-theme wine called "14 Hands," amid a luxe ranch-lodge setting of hardwood floors, rock fireplaces, glittering chandeliers and handcarved wood furnishings.

MUST STAY

Tubac Golf Resort & Spa
$$ **98 rooms and suites**
1 Avenue de Otero, Tubac. 520-398-2211. www.tubacgolfresort.com.
This location has its own golf school around its 27-hole course. But the former 500-acre Otero family hacienda is now first-and-foremost a historic Spanish Colonial retreat. Rooms with archways have wood and tile accents. A 4,000sq ft spa relaxes body and soul with local products. **Stables Ranch Grille ($$$)** shines with steaks, seafood and Mexican fare, including buffalo short rib ragout over pappardelle.

WESTERN ARIZONA

Expensive

Heat Hotel
$$$$ **25 rooms**
1420 MCculloch Blvd. N., Lake Havasu City. 928-854-1130 or 888-898-4328. www.heathotel.com.
This ultra-chic high-rise hotel sits along the channel that flows under the London Bridge. All rooms save one have a balcony overlooking the famous span, but all come with luxury linens, comfortable beds and spacious baths. The 🛏 **patio bar** glows weeknights with pink-neon canopies over plush daybeds. Restaurants are a mere walk away.

UTAH CANYONLANDS

Luxury

Amangiri
$$$$$ **34 suites**
1 Kayenta Rd., Canyon Point, Utah. 435-675-3999.
www.amanresorts.com.
You access the remote property from nearby Page and Lake Powell. Then comes into view an isolated oasis of luxury stretching over a 600-acre desert long populated only by Navajo and Hopi, in the valley of the Grand Staircase-Escalante National Monument. In the rooms, floor-to-ceiling windows draw in canyon views, while private sky lounges invite stargazing. The spa features a floatation therapy pavilion, water pavilion and yoga pavilion. Dining is in the property's sole restaurant, on wood-fired, American and Mediterranean cuisine.

Living room, Amangiri

©Amanresorts

HOTELS

GUEST RANCHES

Modern dude ranches are all about connecting with the trail horses, savoring the remarkable outdoors, and leaving time for human "rebooting" with ultra-comfy accommodations and amenities like hot tubs and chef-caliber meals.

⛺ Rancho de los Caballeros

$$$$$ 79 casitas
1551 S. Vulture Mine Rd., Wickenburg. 928-684-5484. ranchodeloscaballeros.com. Closed mid-May–mid-Oct.
This historic, Territorial-style ranch resort has such a long history that its regulars have "their" casita, and guest horses have "their" stalls. When not trail riding over 20,000 acres (on one of the 100 ranch horses), visitors play golf, swim in the pool, enjoy spa treatments, and partake of cookout suppers in the desert, or a meal in the lodge dining room. A full American plan includes three Southwestern meals daily, like tortilla soup, scallops over white beans and corn, or house-smoked pork chop with three-cheese macaroni for dinner.

⛺ Tanque Verde Ranch

$$$$$ 76 rooms
14301 E. Speedway Blvd., Tucson. 520-296-6275 or 800-234-3833. www.tanqueverderanch.com.
Situated beside Saguaro National Park, the ranch was founded in 1868 on 640 acres in the Rincon Mountains. Stays at this plush, all-inclusive retreat include unlimited riding, cowboy barbecues and Mexican fiestas. Sante Fe-style rooms come with fireplaces or private patios. Pink-stucco casitas and cacti surround the main house, where guests linger over rustic communal tables, or grab a beer at the Doghouse Saloon. The spa embraces local, organic plants and herbs in its treatments.

⛺ Flying E Ranch

$$$$ 14 rooms, 3 suites
2801 W. Wickenburg Way, Wickenburg. 928-684-2690. www. flyingeranch.com. Closed May–Oct.
This working cattle ranch harkens back to old cowboy days on the desert foothills near Vulture Peak and Vulture Gold Mine. Built in 1946, the Western style rooms

Rancho de los Caballeros

include wet bars and refrigerators. A heated pool and hot tub beckon at the end of a glorious day in the saddle. American comfort meals are served family style in the main lodge, with drinks in the saloon. Beginner and advanced trail rides *(exta charge)* explore the 20,000-acre property.

Sunglow Ranch

$$$$ **11 casitas**
14066 S. Sunglow Rd., Pearce. 520-824-3334. www.sunglow ranch.com.

It's like having a private preserve, sprawled over 475 acres in the Chiricahua Mountains next to the 200,000-acre Coronado National Forest, east of Benson. Casitas are rustic territorial and entirely heartwarming, featuring hand-painted murals, fireplaces and patios. Rates include breakfast and a three-course American dinner. Hiking, mountain biking, canoeing, and **stargazing** with a resident astronomer keep guests engaged.

White Stallion Ranch

$$$$ **41 rooms and suites plus a 4-bedroom hacienda**
9251 W. Twin Peaks Rd., Tucson. 520-297-0252. www.white stallion.com.

Since its inception in 1965, this guest ranch has expanded from 200 to 3,000 acres. The land originally was a cattle ranch in the early 1900s, complete with a Mexican adobe lodge (now part of the dining room). Regulars love the all-inclusive goodies like three buffet/grill meals, Southwestern-style rooms, and extra riding daily. Tennis, basketball and volleyball courts, a heated pool, hot tub,

movie theater, games room, petting zoo, fitness center and sauna keep guests busy.

Apache Spirit Ranch

$$$ **17 rooms plus a 4-bedroom hacienda**
895 W. Monument Rd., Tombstone. 520-457-7299 or 877-404-7262. www.apachespiritranch.com.

At the heart of this 272-acre preserve is a faux 1881 frontier town whose main street features the "Old Trappmann" saloon and dining hall, a restaurant, and guesthouses decorated inside-and-out in themes like Blacksmith Shop, Jail, Post Office and Bordello. Built in 2010, the all-inclusive ranch offers modern luxury and plenty of fun with two dozen trusty horses for trailrides along the Dragoon Mountains, and gourmet chuckwagon cookouts (ahi tuna, even). For extra whimsy, there are lasso lessons, bonfire sing-alongs and staged gunfights, as well as a swimming pool.

Saguaro Lake Ranch

$$ **25 cabins plus a 4-bedroom hacienda**
13020 Bush Hwy., Mesa. 480-984-2194. www.saguarolakeranch.com.

The main draw is horseback riding fall through spring, and kayaking and tubing the Salt River in summer (and swimming in the pool). Year-round, the sight of the Sonoran desert and the Goldfield Mountains is stunning. Founded in 1930, the lodge features a four-sided stone fireplace and wagon-wheel lights, while guest quarters are simply furnished with Western accents. The American plan means breakfast, lunch and dinner; the B&B plan covers breakfast only.

GRAND CANYON & ARIZONA

INDEX